D0598086

# NEEDLEPOINT DESIGNS FROM ASIA

*Japanese Flying Pheasant Pillow*

# NEEDLEPOINT DESIGNS FROM ASIA

## 30 EXOTIC DESIGNS FROM PERSIA, INDIA, KOREA, CHINA, AND JAPAN

## GAY ANN ROGERS

DOUBLEDAY & COMPANY, INC., GARDEN CITY, NEW YORK
1983

*Books by Gay Ann Rogers*

Tribal Designs for Needlepoint

An Illustrated History of Needlework Tools

Needlepoint Designs from Asia

## ACKNOWLEDGMENTS

Several people have been particularly helpful in assisting me with this book and I want to mention their specific contributions for which I am very grateful.

I want to thank Jane Stevens for the classes I have taken from her over the years both at the Royal School of Needlework and privately. From the stimulation of her classes, I was able to formulate my own ideas about various graphing techniques and the use of decorative stitches.

Deek Kelley shared with me her many good ideas about the various techniques particularly useful in designing needlepoint graphs.

Anne Marron spent countless hours placing dots with admirable precision on my needlepoint graphs. While Kathy Knotts-Lavine had preferred to draw x's when she helped me with the graphs for *Tribal Designs for Needlepoint*, Anne concentrated on dots—thousands of them.

Peggy Crull designed the shapes for the three purses to fit my needlepoint designs. She then finished the purses and glasses cases with extraordinary skill and care. Finally, she not only gave me many excellent suggestions for the finishing instructions but she double-checked that section as well.

Sandy Higgins once again did the finishing work for many of the projects in this book such as the rugs, the bell pulls, and several of the pillows. They all benefited from her careful attention.

Karen Van Westering, my editor at Doubleday, and Anne Sweeney, her assistant, have consistently been helpful with their thoughtful suggestions and sage advice.

Finally, I must thank my husband, Jim, for his continuing and good-humored support of my work on this book.

BOOK DESIGN BY BEVERLEY VAWTER GALLEGOS

*Library of Congress Cataloging in Publication Data*
*Rogers, Gay Ann.   Needlepoint designs from Asia.*
*1. Canvas embroidery—Asia—Patterns.     I. Title.*
*TT778.C3R59   1983     746.44'2041'095*
*ISBN 0-385-14838-0*
*Library of Congress Catalog Card Number 81–43067*

*In memory of*

*Ceneth Robertson Ross,*

*who traveled
along the silk road
before me*

# CONTENTS

## DESIGNING YOUR OWN CANVASES

## FINISHING THE PROJECT

## APPENDIX

# INTRODUCTION

Several years ago when my husband and I were traveling from Japan and the east coast of Asia to its west coast at Istanbul, we crossed several times the historic "silk road" which linked, through caravans of spices, silks, and other luxuries, the dominant cultures of Asia to each other and to Europe in the Middle Ages. As we wandered through Asia, visiting temples, tombs, museums, and other monuments, I was fascinated by the essential unity of Asian art.

A Korean tomb painting of a royal hunting party bears a striking resemblance in line, color, and style to the same subject on an Indian miniature painting or on a Persian carpet. There are, of course, regional and national differences which accentuate different colors or lines or aspects of style. Beneath these differences, however, is a common cultural substratum which reveals the historic interplay of Asian cultures.

Commerce, mass migrations, invasions from the West by the armies of Islam and from the East by those of the Mongols, the spread of Buddhism eastward from India, and the natural intermixture at cultural borders resulted in a powerful interpenetration of the various Asian cultures over many centuries, creating diversity within unity.

This is not, of course, unusual. When we speak of Gothic art, or of Art Nouveau style in Europe, we are discussing pan-European movements which have general European unifying characteristics at the same time that they reveal to the discriminating eye pronounced regional and national variations. The division of Asia into Near East, Middle East, and Far East is culturally as misleading as the same divisions we make for Western, Central, and Eastern Europe. They are all different in some ways but they are different within a larger and more important cultural unity.

In this book of Asian designs adapted for needlepoint, I have tried to show that essential unity of Asian art. I hope to take the reader on our own "silk road" journey through Asia to view the different regional artifacts which are so adaptable to needlepoint, and so harmonious with one another as well as with Western art.

Because most of us are familiar with Oriental rugs, I have started with a Kazak rug and traveled eastward in these pages through Asia, stopping wherever there is an artifact of interest, whether it be in northern Persia, southern India, or the foothills of the Himalayas. Our final destination, the most eastern terminus of Asia, is Japan.

I hope that this journey will ignite an interest in designing your own canvases and that you will see, from this adaptation of the arabesque and geometric forms of Asian art to needlepoint, that it is possible to adapt a wide range of designs for canvas.

To help you with the graphed projects in this book, I have included in the Getting Started section the necessary information to stitch the graphed designs in the book or to make your own variations on these designs.

I have also included in Designing Your Own Canvases something which is not usually found in needlepoint books: a detailed discussion of the steps necessary to draw and graph designs for canvas. Here I explore the intricacies of lines, curves, and circles as well as choosing and planning for decorative stitches, all with references to the graphed designs included in the book as examples of the points being explained.

Finally, in the last section, I suggest how you may finish all of the projects in this book if you do not want to use a professional finisher.

The Appendix contains diagrams of the stitches needed to complete the projects in this book.

GAY ANN ROGERS

# GETTING STARTED

*Persian Rose and Nightingale Pillow*

# SUPPLIES

Two categories of supplies are described on the following pages: the first includes supplies for stitching the designs in this book; the second has supplies for changing the designs and for designing your own graphs and painted canvases.

## Canvas

There are two varieties and several brands of canvas available on the market today. The two canvas types are penelope and mono. Penelope, a double-thread canvas, has the advantage of allowing the needlewoman to stitch a design partly on the mesh size of 10 stitches per inch, for example, when she covers both threads with one stitch, and partly on the mesh size of 20 stitches per inch when she splits the double threads and covers only one.

Mono canvas, by contrast, is a single-thread canvas, which means that the whole design must be stitched on a single-size mesh. The projects in this book, all relatively uniform in design detail, have been designed for mono canvas.

It is important to select a good-quality canvas which will hold its shape and keep its body much longer than a poorer grade. The more canvas holds its shape, the less distortion there will be from the stitching. A good brand of mono canvas is the German Zweigart, identified by its "redline" selvage and available in most needlepoint shops.

## Threads

At the present time, excellent brands of yarns and threads are available to the needlewoman. Among them are the two brands I have used for the projects in this book. I chose Paternayan yarn and DMC floss and pearl cotton (*perle coton*) for their wide range of colors and easy availability. I do not believe, however, that their quality is markedly any better than other excellent yarns and threads such as Nantucket, Appleton, and Medici.

Paternayan yarn is a 3 ply "Persian-style" yarn. The number of ply the needlewoman uses depends on the mesh size of the canvas although this may vary according to the individual stitcher's tension. In general, the relation of ply to canvas mesh size is as follows: 3 ply covers 10 mesh canvas; 2 ply covers 12 and 14 mesh canvas; 1 ply covers 18 mesh canvas.

DMC pearl cotton is a shiny twisted thread available most frequently in two sizes: ⌗3 and ⌗5. As a rule, ⌗3 pearl cotton covers 14 mesh canvas and ⌗5 pearl cotton covers 18 mesh canvas. In density, 1 strand of ⌗3 pearl cotton equals 2 strands of ⌗5 pearl cotton. DMC pearl cotton is also available in ⌗8, which is very fine.

DMC floss is a 6 ply cotton thread whose coverage depends on the individual stitcher's tension. Generally, 12 ply will cover 14 mesh canvas and 6 ply will cover 18 mesh canvas.

For the Persian Rose and Nightingale pillow, I used gold metallic thread. I chose Christopher's although others equally good are available. Christopher's is a good quality metallic thread for both 14 and 18 mesh canvases and it is easy to use.

## Needles

Needlepoint requires tapestry needles with blunt ends and large eyes for threading yarns. Tapestry needle sizes correspond to canvas mesh sizes as follows: use #18 needles for 10 mesh canvas, #20 needles for 12 mesh canvas, #22 needles for 14 mesh canvas, and #24 needles for 18 mesh canvas.

Needles tarnish easily from hand acids and from exposure to the atmosphere. If needles are not removed from stored needlepoint projects, the needles may stain threads and canvas.

To clean needles, slide them back and forth into an emery cushion until the emery powder scours them clean.

## Thimble

A thimble protects a stitcher's finger from developing holes while pushing needles through canvas. Many stitchers claim that they cannot endure thimbles and proudly wear their finger holes as badges of courageous stitching. Learning to wear a thimble comfortably is an easy process and worth the effort. Choose one that fits snugly but comfortably and leave it on your finger for a day or so whether or not you are stitching. You will soon grow as accustomed to it as if you were wearing a new ring. The next time you wear it, the thimble will not seem awkward.

## Scissors

At one time or another, every needlewoman will have to rip out mistakes. Scissors with sharp points and thin blades make this unwelcome task much easier. Felix scissors or the traditional stork-shaped scissors, both from Solingen, Germany, are suitable for this task.

## Binding for Canvas

To keep the edges of your canvas from unraveling, bind them with cotton bias tape. Use a sewing machine zigzag stitch or a long hand-basting stitch.

Another way to bind the edge is to fold it under approximately ⅜ inch and secure it with a long hand-basting stitch.

## Frames

Two types of frames are available for holding needlepoint canvas taut. One is a set of stretcher bars onto which the canvas is stapled or tacked. The other is a frame with roller bars, commonly called a scroll frame. The canvas is stitched to strips of fabric attached to top and bottom roller bars and then laced to each side. The needlewoman can then roll the canvas not currently being stitched. A flexible floor stand is also available which holds either stretcher bars or a scroll frame and allows the needlewoman to adjust the frame to a comfortable position. The advantage of the floor stand is that it frees both of the needlewoman's hands for stitching.

## Indelible Markers

If you wish to draw on canvas, you must use a pen that is waterproof. If it is not, the ink will bleed and stain yarns and threads when you block your work. One brand of indelible marker suitable for drawing on needlepoint canvas is a Nepo pen, made especially for needlepoint canvas, and available in many needlework shops.

Even if a pen is marked "waterproof," do not trust your work to it without first testing the pen. Draw on a swatch of canvas and allow the ink to dry, then blot the ink with a warm damp towel. If no ink smudges appear on the towel, the ink is most likely waterproof. Because the qualities of waterproofing depend not only on the ink but on the surface receiving the ink, test every different canvas you plan to mark.

## Paint

Several types of paints are suitable for needlepoint canvas. These include acrylic paints, oils, textile paints, and some felt-tip pens. The most simple to use are acrylic paints as they are easily mixed, thinned with water, quick-drying, and waterproof once they are dry. Test each paint tube, particularly black, strong reds, and red blues, to make certain that it is waterproof. Use the same test as for indelible markers above.

## Acrylic Fixative

When you have finished marking or painting canvas, allow it to dry thoroughly. Then spray it on both sides with a clear acrylic fixative as an added precaution against bleeding ink or paint. Clear acrylic fixatives, made by Krylon, Blair, or Grumbacher, are available in most art and hardware stores.

## Brushes

Some beginning painters make the mistake of buying cheap brushes. If you plan to paint several needlepoint canvases, invest in three good-quality brushes. They will improve your painting skills. Although I prefer Grumbacher sable brushes with bright tips (square ends), an old rule suggests using natural bristles for oils and watercolors, and acrylic or nylon brushes for acrylic paint. You might try each to see which you prefer. Good sizes to start with are 00 or 0; 2 or 3; 6, 7, or 8.

## Ruler

The majority of needlepoint projects are larger than the typical household foot ruler. An 18-inch ruler will save you the effort of constantly moving the ruler from one edge of the canvas to the other.

## Drawing Paper

A tablet of bond paper approximately 14 by 17 inches will serve as a good starting paper. It is not as rough as newsprint nor as expensive as good-quality drawing paper.

## Tracing Paper

Tracing paper is an invaluable design aid for many uses. For example, you may decide you like parts of a design but wish to discard other parts. You can trace the parts of the design you like and begin again with those alone.

## Graph Paper

There are two types of graph paper: one with light blue "non-reproducing" lines; another with red, black, orange, or green "reproducing" lines. In reproduction processes, most cameras will not see light blue. The light blue lines will vanish when the design is reproduced. By contrast, red, black, orange, or green lines will reproduce sharply.

Both types of graph paper are useful to the needlepoint designer. For example, non-reproducing graph paper is good for stitch diagrams you want to reproduce. Perhaps a sheet of graph paper has 32 horizontal grid lines and 44 vertical grid lines, but you want to use only 12 by 12 of those grid lines on which to draw your stitch diagram. With non-reproducing paper you can trace the precise number of grid lines you wish to use. The others will magically disappear in the reproduction process. Because the basic construction of grid lines is already drawn, the non-reproducing graph paper will save you the time and effort of spacing, measuring, and constructing your own grid lines. Graph paper 4-to-the-inch is a good choice for such tasks.

The uses of reproducing graph paper are most obvious. If you want to design and then reproduce a graph, you will want not only your symbols but also the grid lines of the graph paper to reproduce well.

Graph paper of both types is available with all grid lines of equal density or with one line (most typically the line marking an inch in space) darkened slightly. For 4-to-the-inch graph paper, the accented line is the 4th line; for 10-to-the-inch graph paper, the accented line is the 10th line. Graph paper with accented inch lines is easier to count.

Graph paper is available in various degrees of quality. Use the quality of paper suitable to your task. For a preliminary graph you would obviously use a lower quality. If, however, you want to do a master copy for reproduction and then save it for later reproduction, use a high-quality, high rag content paper. K & E graph papers are good-quality papers from Keuffel & Esser Co., Morristown, N.J. 07960. They are available in many art and drafting supply shops.

Given the growing popularity of graphs in the stitchery world, it was only a matter of time until someone made available graph paper with grid counts to correspond to the canvas mesh sizes. The company is Needlegraph, and their graph paper is available in many needlework shops.

## Additional Supplies

For designing, graphing, or painting canvases, you will need sharp pencils, felt-tip pens, a good art eraser, a jar for water to thin paints, paper towels, and a palette. A plasticized paper plate or a white ceramic plate covered with transparent vinyl such as Saran Wrap works well as a palette.

# GENERAL INSTRUCTIONS

The instructions with each of the designs in this book give the following information: a history of the design; size of the canvas and the thread count for the design; stitching directions; color and stitch key; and creative alternatives. The directions are often repeated from project to project so that each can be worked without frequent reference to other sections of the book.

## Canvas

Information about canvas includes the thread count for each design along with recommendations for canvas mesh sizes and the resulting dimensions in inches of the project. For most designs, I have suggested two different canvas meshes, with the corresponding size of the piece of canvas required and the finished measurement of the project.

The thread count is the number of meshes that will eventually be stitched along the design at its widest or longest point. For example, the Persian Elephants pillow measures 260 threads at its widest point by 292 threads at its longest point. The thread count of a graphed design remains a constant measurement, while the size of the graphed design in inches will vary according to the mesh size of the canvas. If the Persian Elephants pillow design is worked on 14 mesh canvas, it will measure approximately 18½ by 21 inches; if worked on 18 mesh canvas, the design will measure about 14½ by 16½ inches.

If you want to work any design on a canvas mesh other than the one I have suggested, use the thread count and the following formula to compute the size of a graphed design on different canvas meshes: divide the thread count of the design by the canvas mesh size to determine the size of the project in inches. For example, the Persian Elephants thread count of 260 (width) divided by 10 (the canvas mesh) equals 26 inches; the Persian Elephants thread count of 292 (length) divided by 10 (the canvas mesh) equals approximately 29 inches. If stitched on 10 mesh canvas, the Persian Elephants design would be 26 by 29 inches, a good size for a small rug.

The size of the piece of canvas for the project should not only cover the dimensions of the finished project but also an additional minimum of 1½ inches on all four sides. For example, to stitch the Persian Elephants on 10 mesh canvas requires a piece of canvas 29 by 32 inches for a finished project approximately 26 by 29 inches computed as follows: 1½ + 26 + 1½ = 29 inches; 1½ + 29 + 1½ + 32 inches. The extra 1½ inches of canvas on each side is the *minimum* extra canvas necessary on each side for blocking and finishing the project.

## Stitching Directions

The majority of the designs are graphed in full. A few repeat designs are graphed in part with instructions for repeating the graph to complete the design (see the following section on mirror images). Because of size, many of the graphs are divided into several parts such as quarters or halves. At the beginning of the stitching directions for each design, I have specified the number of pieces in the full graph.

If you examine the graph parts carefully, you will find small arrows just outside the border. Follow the arrows to the points where they intersect; the intersection marks the center of the design. Two typical examples of the arrangements of graph parts and how their centers are marked are illustrated in Figures 1 and 2.

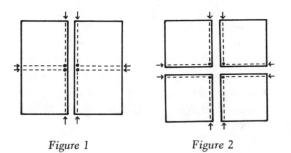

Figure 1          Figure 2

To begin work, mark the center of the graph with a pen or pencil; then mark the center of the canvas with an indelible marker. Now count from the center point of the graph to the border and mark this border on your canvas. Then begin to count as follows: from center to left border; from center to right border; from center to top; from center to bottom. This precautionary measure will ensure that the size of the canvas is adequate for the design.

Each square of the graph represents one stitch on the canvas. To begin stitching, count off the squares of the graph from the center and stitch each corresponding mesh of canvas. When possible, stitch from the center of the graph outward to the border. Stitching from the center point keeps the procedure of your work balanced, allowing you to check and recheck the accuracy of your counting. Working from the center point is particularly helpful when stitching rugs: you will not have to go back through the bulk of a stitched border to fill in a center portion.

Many of the designs have outlines which should be worked first. They will serve as a guide which tells you quickly if your counting is accurate. Working outlines is particularly important if they contain decorative stitches. Once you have established the outlines, you will see the total area for a decorative stitch.

So far, the stitching directions have been for those who want to count a few squares from the graph and then stitch them. There is an alternative to this constant counting while stitching. You can transfer the entire design to canvas before you begin stitching. Count from the graph and mark each corresponding mesh of your canvas with an indelible pen. Use different-colored indelible pens to mark the boundaries where different colors meet.

There are two advantages to this method of work. You will be able to stitch in the midst of distractions since you will have completed all of your counting. You can also paint the canvas, thus providing a base of similar color under dark yarn. This will prevent flecks of white canvas from peeking through dark yarns.

*Mirror Image*

For four designs in this book (East Persian Lions pillow, Tibetan purse, Chinese purse, and Mongol purse), I have graphed only half of the design because the second half of the design is repeated as though reflected in a mirror. The term "mirror image" used in the directions for these designs means a repetition in *reverse* of the graphed design. See Figure 3 (A is the mirror image of B).

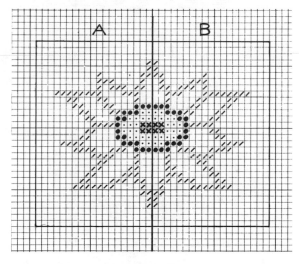

Figure 3

For four other designs (Kazak rug, Japanese Imari pillow, the borders of the North Persian Earthenware pillow, and Persian rug), I have graphed only one fourth of the design because the second quarter is repeated in a mirror image of the first, and then the two quarters together, which equal one half, are repeated in a mirror image to complete the design. See Figures 4, 5, and 6.

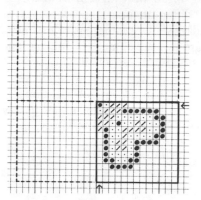

*Figure 4*

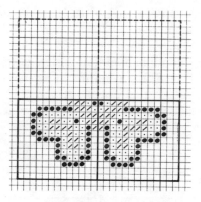

*Figure 5*

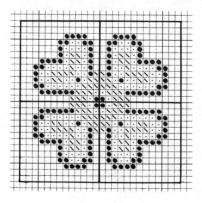

*Figure 6*

## Color and Stitch Key

The symbols on each graph indicate different colors and often different decorative stitches. The color and stitch key provides the name of the color and the color number for the type of yarn or thread suggested.

For example: ⬤ Charcoal gray, Paternayan yarn #221.

The key often gives the name of a decorative stitch. If no stitch name appears opposite the graph symbol, use Basketweave of Continental stitch. If you are unfamiliar with the name of a certain stitch, there is an alphabetical glossary of stitch diagrams in the Appendix at the end of the book.

The colors and decorative stitches I suggest are only recommendations. You may want to experiment with other color combinations and decorative stitches as well.

## Creative Alternatives

Rather than regarding the designs for this book as fixed patterns, I look at them as starting points for experimentation. The Creative Alternatives section of the instructions suggests different ways of treating each design. It suggests that no design must be reproduced exactly as presented. Nor are these alternatives the only possibilities for changing the design.

## Yarn Count

To determine how much yarn or thread is necessary to complete a needlepoint project is guesswork at best. It depends not only on the size of the canvas and the number of ply, but also on individual tension, stitching habits, and the different decorative stitches used. In addition, you must consider the changes and mistakes you may make as you proceed.

Rather than listing specific amounts of yarn or thread for each project, I suggest a method for determining the quantity needed. First, buy your canvas and mark the center and borders with an indelible marker. With the help of a needlepoint shop, you will now be able to decide approximately how much yarn you will need for the total project.

Next, study the graph and decide which color or colors you will begin using first. If the design calls for outlines, begin with the outlining colors. Taking into account the maximum amount of yarn you need to complete the whole project, guess what proportion of the starting color you might use. For example, if the design requires a total of 8 ounces, you might begin with 1 or 2 ounces of the outlining color.

As you stitch and the design evolves you will be able to guess more accurately about the quantity needed for the remaining colors. When in question, err on the side of too much rather than too little yarn. An ounce or two of extra yarn, allowing you to complete the design with a single dye lot of each color, is vastly preferable to 3 strands too few, forcing you to introduce a second dye lot of a color.

In a genuine emergency, where you are irrevocably caught with an insufficient amount of yarn, you can use a second dye lot of a color as long as the second dye lot is not contiguous to the first. Most colors in a given design are broken by a second color with the exception usually of the background color. Consequently, it is best to leave your background color until last when you can make your most accurate prediction about the quantity of yarn needed.

This method for choosing yarns does not imply that you should choose colors one by one. Quite on the contrary, you should decide on your colors as a group. The choice of one color influences the choice of another, and the two in turn influence the choice of a third. When you decide on a group of colors, keep a record of the color numbers and then begin with one or two, buying the others later.

## Stitching Techniques

The following are a few simple techniques which may help improve the quality of your stitching:

1. When using Basketweave stitch, always start and end the thread on the straight grain or cross grain of the canvas. Do not follow the diagonal line created by the stitching as this will increase the possibility of ridges in your work.

2. Today's yarns often vary in circumference from ply to ply and strand to strand, creating a thick and thin appearance. Examine each strand of yarn before using it and choose only those strands or portions of strands uniform in size.

3. Atmospheric acids or those from your skin may cause needles to tarnish. Discard tarnished needles or clean them with emery powder. A smooth, clean needle glides much more easily and accurately between stitches.

4. Whenever possible, try to finish stitching a given area in one sitting. Your tension may change slightly from one stitching session to another, producing a noticeable difference in stitches, particularly in long rows of Basketweave.

5. When working decorative stitches over 3 or 4 meshes or more, use a looser than normal tension so that you do not pull the canvas threads together in clumps. For example, Scotch stitch and Rhodes stitch, like most Block and Cross stitches, tend to pull canvas threads together under each stitch unit, leaving exposed threads and spaces between stitches.

6. Try to stitch with a thread no longer than 18 inches. Constant friction created by pulling thread through the canvas often thins the yarn toward the end of a strand. If you must stitch with a long thread, check constantly to see that the thread remains consistent in size. Discard it if it shows signs of wear.

7. Even if you use short threads, do not stitch to the very end of the thread where the bend through the needle's eye causes wear.

8. DMC pearl cotton often loses its luster toward the end of the strand. Watch carefully for this and end off the strand as soon as you notice a lack of luster. DMC floss may do the same.

9. If you use more than 1 ply of yarn or thread, separate the ply and then put them back together. Straighten each stitch as you pull the yarn through the canvas so that the ply lie side by side without twists in the yarn. Unnecessary yarn twists cause irregularity in the appearance of your work.

10. Every few stitches or rows of stitches, drop your needle, letting the needle and yarn hang freely. This allows the yarn to untwist, ridding itself of twists accumulated as you stitch.

11. Mount and work your canvas on a frame

whenever you plan to use several ply of yarn or floss, or whenever you plan to use decorative stitches pulled over many canvas meshes. The frame will allow you to use both hands to straighten yarn ply for each stitch. It will also help you regulate your tension for stitches over many canvas meshes.

12. If your tension is tight or uneven, the use of a frame for all projects will help the appearance of your work.

13. When using decorative stitches, always begin and end each stitch unit at the same points and make certain that the steps used in creating stitch units follow the same progression from stitch to stitch. This is particularly important for uniformity of various Cross stitches and Rhodes stitch.

14. Pay attention to accurate stitch compensation. When you cannot complete a full stitch unit because another area of the design interferes, determine just how much of the stitch you can complete. Keep the yarn direction of each partial stitch unit consistent with the yarn direction of full stitch units. If the stitch unit employs two or three color values, keep the colors used in a partial stitch unit consistent with colors of full stitch units. If you do not compensate carefully, the effect, on close scrutiny, will be muddy and confusing to the eye.

# THE DESIGNS

*Kazak Rug*

# KAZAK RUG

## History

The design for this rug is adapted from Kazak rugs made in the southwest region of the Caucasus. The designs for these rugs are geometric with large and bold medallions against a background covered with smaller ornamental designs and surrounded by white and multicolored borders, often with linked and spike-like designs. The colors are bright and limited. The Kazak nomads and villagers usually made small rugs, about 3 by 5 feet, known as *zaronim* because of their size. The robust and hardy quality of these rugs made them popular in Western countries from an early time.

## Canvas

The thread count for the design is 388 threads wide by 628 threads long.

If you choose 10 mesh canvas, cut and bind a piece of canvas 42 by 66 inches for a finished design approximately 39 by 63 inches.

If you choose 12 mesh canvas, cut and bind a piece of canvas 35½ by 55½ inches for a finished design approximately 32½ by 52½ inches.

## Stitching Directions

The rug graph is drawn in two parts—Graphs A and B. Together, the two parts equal the lower right quarter of the finished design. See Figure 7.

Find and mark the center of your canvas with an indelible marker. Follow the two arrows marked at the edges of the graph parts until they intersect.

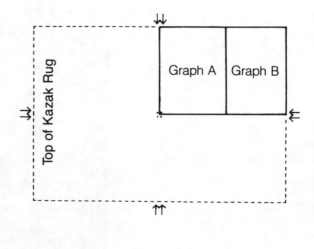

Figure 7

This square corresponds to the center of your canvas and marks the place you will begin stitching.

From the center point of your canvas, count 194 threads (half the horizontal thread count) toward the right and mark this edge lightly on your canvas. Returning to the center point, count 314 threads (half the vertical thread count) toward the bottom and mark this edge lightly on your canvas. These are the right and bottom edges of the design.

You are now ready to begin stitching. Counting from the center points, stitch Graph A. Then stitch Graph B in its appropriate place beneath Graph A, as indicated in Figure 7. You have now completed the lower right quarter of the design.

Stitch the lower left quarter of the rug in a mirror image of the lower right quarter. You have now completed the lower half of the rug. Stitch the upper half of the rug in a mirror image of the lower half.

Stitch the entire design in Continental or Basketweave stitch.

## Color Key

The original rug was red, blue, black, gold, and white. I changed the red to rust, the blue to green, and the black to charcoal gray. Yarn numbers refer to Paternayan yarn. See Plate 1.

*Figure 8*

*Figure 9*

*Figure 10*

## Creative Alternatives

DESIGN CHANGES: You can adapt many of the rug motifs for different projects. The center of the rug will make a pillow on 14 or 18 mesh canvas. A small portion of the border can be used for a glasses case. Any of the three illustrated motifs will make a pincushion. Combine and alternate them for a bell pull. See Figures 8, 9, and 10.

COLOR CHANGES: For a predominantly green rug, reverse the green and rust so that the background of the rug is green.

To do the rug in its original colors, change the color key as follows: charcoal gray to black (※220

Paternayan yarn), green to blue (※500 or ※501), rust to red (※840); gold and white remain the same. This will make a predominantly red rug; for a predominantly blue rug, reverse the red and blue so that the background is blue.

For a black, brown, gray, and white rug, change the color key as follows: charcoal gray to black (※220), green to gray (※202), gold to light gray (※203), rust to brown (※411); white remains the same.

STITCH CHANGES: For best wear, a rug should be stitched in Continental or Basketweave stitch. Most decorative stitches carry the thread over 2 or more meshes. The longer the thread, the more easily it will wear. If, however, you are using any of the motifs for a pillow, pincushion, or bell pull, you can then experiment with decorative stitches.

*Graph A*

☑ GREEN #662    ⟋ GOLD #733    ☐ RUST #871

*Graph B*

# TURKISH GLASSES CASE

## History

The design for this glasses case is a free adaptation from a Turkish tile of the late sixteenth century. The bold design is typical of this genre of tile, which came largely from Iznik. These tiles were made of a grayish fired clay covered with very white tin-glaze slip. Sometimes, as here, a brilliant blue partially covered the white ground, producing an abstract design. The tiles were often produced in multiples to create wall panels which might span 12 feet.

## Canvas

The thread count for the design is 70 threads wide by 122 threads long. Cut and bind two pieces of 18 mesh canvas each 7 by 10 inches for finished designs approximately 4 by 7 inches.

## Stitching Directions

Follow the arrows marked at the edges of the graph to find the four center squares. Mark the 4 center meshes of each piece of canvas with an indelible marker to correspond to the four center squares on the graph. From the center points, count outward and lightly mark the left, right, top, and bottom edges of the design on each piece of canvas.

You are now ready to begin stitching. Counting from the center points, stitch the design on one piece of canvas. Stitch the entire design in Continental or Basketweave stitch. Repeat the design in a mirror image on the second piece of canvas. You have now completed the front and back of the glasses case.

## Color and Stitch Key

The colors are close to those of the original tile. Yarn numbers refer to Paternayan yarn. The location of the stitches used is noted on the key. See Plate 9.

## Creative Alternatives

DESIGN CHANGES: Using the graph as a horizontal pattern, you can make a small pillow on 10 mesh canvas. Increase the size of the background area.

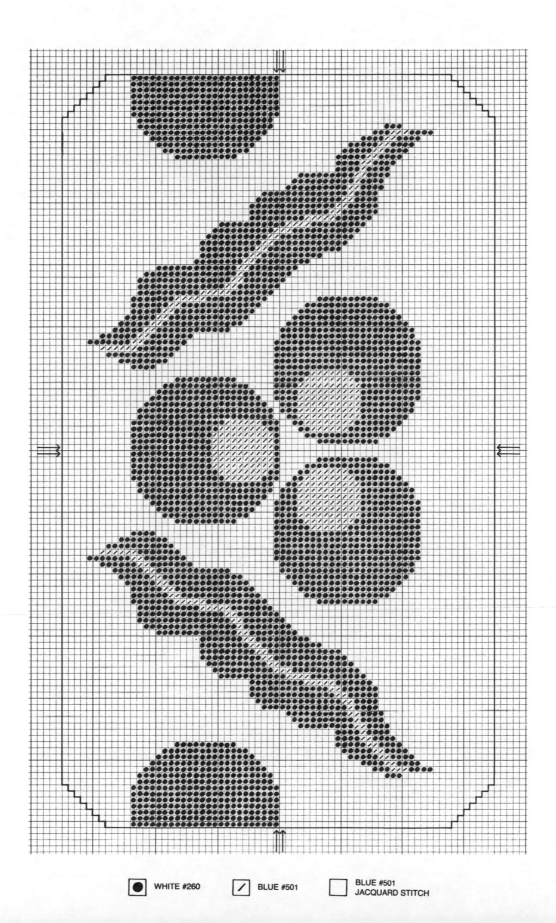

● WHITE #260     ╱ BLUE #501     ☐ BLUE #501
                                    JACQUARD STITCH

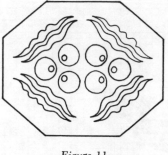

*Figure 11*

To make a pillow using a variation of the design, stitch the design and then repeat it in a mirror image. Omit the half circles at the edges. The pillow can be square or octagonal as in Figure 11.

COLOR CHANGES: Reverse the white and blue so that the circles and lines are blue and the background is white. You can make a pillow or rug by combining several panels of the design stitched in alternating color patterns. The first would be white on blue, the second blue on white, the third white on blue, etc.

Any two colors can be substituted for blue and white. If you decide to make a rug by combining panels of this design, you could choose several colors and change the color combination for each panel.

STITCH CHANGES: The simple design lends itself to a large-scale decorative stitch for the background. If you increase the size of the background area, you could try Tile stitch in three colors or Crossed Corners stitch in two colors. Any diagonal stitch would also work well.

# NORTH PERSIAN EARTHENWARE PILLOW

## History

The design for this pillow is adapted from an alkaline-glazed earthenware plate painted in black underglaze. It was made in North Persia in the first half of the sixteenth century. The original plate is about the same size, 13 inches in diameter, as the pillow. This design is typical of North Persian pottery of this period where the animal forms (the two fish) are usually subordinate elements to a larger, ornamental design. By the early sixteenth century, such designs had become delicate and complex, and the animal forms were usually presented as though they were in lively motion.

## Canvas

The thread count for the design is 236 threads in diameter.

If you choose 14 mesh canvas, cut and bind a piece of canvas 20 inches square for a finished design approximately 17 inches in diameter.

If you choose 18 mesh canvas, cut and bind a piece of canvas 16 inches square for a finished design approximately 13 inches in diameter.

## Stitching Directions

The design is represented by a two-part graph. The first part, Graph A, is the center of the design. The second part, Graph B, is the lower right quarter of the border. Figure 12 demonstrates how the two parts fit together.

Follow the arrows marked at the edges of Graph A to find the four center squares on the graph. Find and mark the center 4 meshes of your canvas with an indelible marker to correspond to the center of Graph A. Counting from the center points to the right, then left, then top, then bottom, lightly mark the canvas so that the diameter measures 236 threads.

You are now ready to begin stitching. First, stitch Graph A. Counting from the center outward, stitch the charcoal gray fish and then fill in the light blue background.

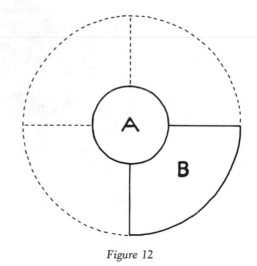

*Figure 12*

Now stitch Graph B, fitting the lower right quarter of the border against the lower right quarter of Graph A. Stitch the lower left quarter of the border in a mirror image of the lower right quarter. You will now have completed the lower half of the border. Stitch the upper half of the border in a mirror image of the lower right half.

Stitch the entire design in Continental or Basketweave stitch.

## Color Key

The colors of the original design were a bright blue-green and black. I changed the bright blue-green to light blue, and the black to charcoal gray. Yarn numbers refer to Paternayan yarn. See Plate 2.

## Creative Alternatives

DESIGN CHANGES: Replace the fish design from the center of the pillow with a monogram or single initial. Stitch a smaller round pillow by eliminating the outer two rings of the border (the script and the trellis), leaving only a monogram surrounded by flowers. See Figure 13.

COLOR CHANGES: Any two colors of sufficient contrast will work well for this design. Try blue (in place of charcoal gray) and white (in place of blue).

*Figure 13*

STITCH CHANGES: The design is sufficiently busy that use of decorative stitches will detract from the pillow. If you wish to use a decorative stitch, try Mosaic or St. George and St. Andrew Cross stitch in all charcoal gray areas.

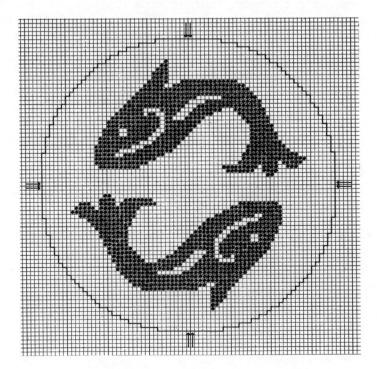

*Graph A*

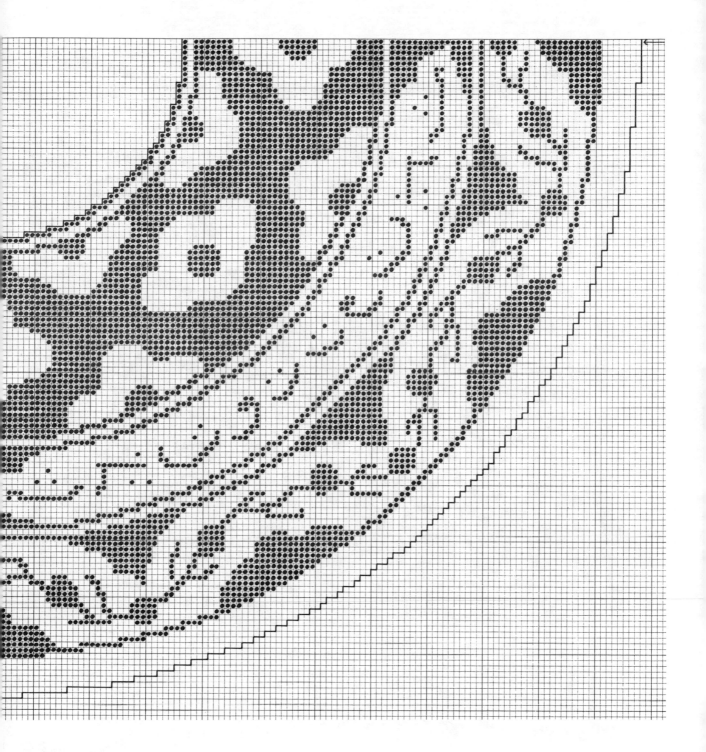

● CHARCOAL GRAY #221     □ BLUE #504

*Graph B*

*Persian Elephants Pillow*

# PERSIAN ELEPHANTS PILLOW

## History

The design for this pillow is adapted from a thirteenth-century Persian scientific treatise called *The Book of the Usefulness of Animals*. It is a commentary in the manner of the first-century Greek physician Dioscorides, who wrote *De Materia Medica* on the usefulness of healing substances found in plants. This work became known to the Persians and reflects the tradition of Arabic translations and commentaries on classical Greek and Latin texts in science and philosophy. The charming animation of the mother elephant tending her young owes nothing, however, to antiquity, but reflects the unique Persian tradition of portraying animals. This particular volume was painted and assembled at the end of the thirteenth century.

## Canvas

The thread count for the design is 260 threads by 292 threads.

If you choose 14 mesh canvas, cut and bind a piece of canvas 21½ by 24 inches for a finished design approximately 18½ by 21 inches.

If you choose 18 mesh canvas, cut and bind a piece of canvas 17½ by 19½ inches for a finished design approximately 14½ by 16½ inches.

## Stitching Directions

The graph is drawn in quarters—Upper Left, Upper Right, Lower Left, or Lower Right according to its position in relation to the whole design.

Follow the two arrows marked at the edges of each graph quarter until they intersect. This intersection marks the square on each quarter where you should begin stitching. Together, the four squares, one from each quarter, mark the center of the design.

Find and mark the center 4 meshes of your canvas with an indelible marker to correspond to the four center squares of the graph. From these center points, count outward and lightly mark the edges of the design on the canvas.

You are now ready to begin stitching. Counting from the center outward, stitch the charcoal gray outlines of the elephants and the gold border outlines. Then fill in the various colors and details of

CHARCOAL GRAY #221    MEDIUM BLUE #504    LIGHT PURPLE #313    GREEN #612

GRAY #202    LIGHT BLUE #505    RED #841    LIGHT GREEN #613

*Upper Left*    DARK BLUE #502    PURPLE #312    ORANGE #800    GREEN #612, LIGHT GREEN #613 DOUBLE CROSS STITCH

*Upper Right*

*Lower Left*

*Lower Right*

the elephants. Stitch the flowers, stems, and leaves and then the grass. Next, work the lettering and then the Scotch stitch and St. George and St. Andrew Cross stitch borders. Finally, stitch the lettering background and the Diagonal Mosaic stitch background.

## Color and Stitch Key

The colors are approximately those used in the original painting. Yarn numbers refer to Paternayan yarn. The location of decorative stitches is noted on the key. The key instructs you to stitch the grass in green and light green Double Cross stitch. Refer to the Double Cross stitch diagrams; work step 1 in green and step 2 in light green. The key also instructs you to stitch the outer border in white and light gold St. George and St. Andrew Cross stitch. Refer to the St. George and St. Andrew Cross stitch diagrams; stitch step 1 in light gold and step 2 in white. See Plate 11.

## Creative Alternatives

DESIGN CHANGES: For a smaller pillow, stitch only the area of the elephants, flowers, and grass in-side the first gold border line, omitting all border areas. Add 1 inch of background.

For a different pillow, omit all border areas, but extend the background area 1 inch toward the top and 2 to 4 inches to the left and right. Add a sprinkling of flowers, leaves, and stems and extend the grass to the edges.

For still another pillow, change the border around the elephants in the following way: leave in place the row of gold Slanting Gobelin stitch around the elephants; to this add 8 rows (32 stitches) of light gold Scotch stitch. This omits the second gold border, all script, and the St. George and St. Andrew Cross stitch border.

COLOR CHANGES: For predominantly purple and gray elephants instead of blue and gray ones, reverse the purple and blue areas of the elephants in the following way: stitch the baby elephant in purple (✳312 Paternayan yarn) and light purple (✳313); change the light blue of the mother elephant to pale purple (✳314); stitch both elephants' ears in dark blue (✳502) and medium blue (✳504).

STITCH CHANGES: Change the light gold Scotch stitch border to light gold Rhodes stitch over 4 meshes.

Stitch the entire border in rows of gold Slanting Gobelin stitch.

# PERSIAN ROSE AND NIGHTINGALE PILLOW

## History

The design for this pillow is adapted from a late eighteenth-century Persian painting. The unknown artist used gouache on paper to render this scene. The careful attention to details of line and hue in the original painting suggests the training characteristic of Persian painters in the use of color and in drawing. The choice of the rose as subject is not surprising since it is not only the oldest domesticated flower but the one most often associated with love and happiness in the Near East as well as the West.

## Canvas

The thread count for the design is 244 threads wide by 312 threads long.

If you choose 14 mesh canvas, cut and bind a piece of canvas 20½ by 25½ inches for a finished design approximately 17½ by 22½ inches.

If you choose 18 mesh canvas, cut and bind a piece of canvas 16½ by 20½ inches for a finished design 13½ by 17½ inches.

## Stitching Directions

The graph is drawn in quarters—Upper Left, Upper Right, Lower Left, or Lower Right according to its position in relation to the whole design.

Follow the two arrows marked at the edges of each graph quarter until they intersect. This intersection marks the square on each quarter where you should begin stitching. Together the four squares, one from each quarter, mark the center of the design.

Find and mark the center 4 meshes of your canvas with an indelible marker to correspond to the four center squares of the graph. From these center points, count outward and lightly mark the edges of the design on the canvas.

Because of the multiple strands of DMC floss and the length of the border stitches, this project should be stitched on a frame. (See Stitching Techniques.) Mount the canvas on a suitable frame checking to see that it is taut. (See Frames.)

You are now ready to begin stitching. Counting from the center outward, stitch the black, red, and metallic gold border outlines. Next, stitch the nightingale, roses, branches, and leaves. Then stitch the lettering and fill in the lettering background. Work the small border of white Tied Cross stitch and then the bottom border of light gold Rhodes stitches over 8 meshes. Next, stitch the 9 large Rhodes stitches over 12 meshes on the side and top borders, then the Rhodes stitches over 4 meshes, and finally the Fern stitch rows, all in light gold. Last, work the medium blue, light blue, and metallic gold Scotch stitch, the black Cross stitch border, and then the white Oriental stitch background.

*Upper Left*

BLACK #310

BLACK #310
SLANTING GOBELIN STITCH OVER 2 MESHES

BLACK #310
CROSS STITCH

DARK GRAY #844

MEDIUM GRAY #318

LIGHT GRAY #415

DARK GREEN #367

MEDIUM GREEN #320

LIGHT GREEN #368

|  |  |
|--------|-------|
| ● RED #349 | |
| ⊞ DARK CORAL #351 | |
| ∨ MEDIUM CORAL #353 | |
| ╲ LIGHT CORAL #948 | |
| Z BROWN #640 | |
| I WHITE BLANC NEIGE | |
| · WHITE BLANC NEIGE ORIENTAL STITCH | |
| L WHITE BLANC NEIGE TIED CROSS STITCH | |
| N WHITE BLANC NEIGE SCOTCH STITCH OVER 4 MESHES | |

*Upper Right*

*Lower Left*

*Lower Right*

## Color and Stitch Key

The colors are approximately those used in the original painting. Thread numbers refer to DMC 6-strand floss and metallic gold thread. The location of various decorative stitches is noted on the key. The key instructs you to use medium blue and light blue floss and metallic gold for the Scotch stitch border. Referring to the diagrams of Scotch stitch using three colors, work step 1 with medium blue floss, step 2 with light blue floss, and step 3 with metallic gold thread. See Plate 6.

## Creative Alternatives

DESIGN CHANGES: Stitch the rose and nightingale as a small pillow by omitting all of the border.

Or stitch the rose and nightingale, using the light gold and white portions of the border but omitting the blue and metallic gold Scotch stitch and black Cross stitch portions of the border.

You can also use the border independently as a border for another design. Omit the rose and nightingale and substitute a monogram of blue and gold.

If you want to omit the script, stitch those three areas using Rhodes stitches and Fern stitches as in the light gold top and side panels.

COLOR CHANGES: If you prefer not to work with metallic thread, use dark blue floss (✳924 DMC floss) instead.

The border would also be effective stitched in green. In place of light gold, use light green (✳368). Instead of white Tied Cross, use pale green (✳369); in place of light blue and medium blue, use light green (✳368) and medium green (✳320) with metallic gold for the Scotch stitch border. Do not change the black, red, and metallic gold parts of the border.

STITCH CHANGES: Use Diagonal Mosaic stitch in place of Oriental stitch for the white background.

In place of the Fern stitch in the light gold border panels, you might use Rhodes stitches over 4 meshes. You can either keep the 3 Rhodes stitches over 12 meshes at the center of each of these panels or omit them, making the whole panel a series of Rhodes stitches over 4 meshes.

Instead of the blue Scotch stitch border, you might use a straight stitch such as Hungarian or Double Hungarian stitch. Miter the corners so that the stitch changes directions correctly. Vary the two blues and gold metallic thread, either row by row or stitch unit by stitch unit.

# PERSIAN GLASSES CASE

## History

The design for this glasses case is a free adaptation of a detail from a Persian miniature painted in Shiraz in the fifteenth century. The miniature was commissioned for a manuscript on the life of the ruler Timur depicting his triumphal entry into conquered Samarkand. The case captures the spirit of geometric detail which permeates much of the ornamentation in Persian miniatures. Abstract stylized representations of flora and fauna form the basis of much of the geometric detail. In this particular case, the abstract design within the geometric medallion probably derives from a flower gradually stylized into a geometric form. The medallion itself is a typical pattern found in many forms of Persian art of this period.

## Canvas

The thread count for the design is 62 threads wide by 110 threads long. Cut and bind two pieces of 18 mesh canvas each 6½ by 9½ inches for a finished design approximately 3½ by 6½ inches.

## Stitching Directions

The graph is drawn in two parts, the back and front of the glasses case. The measurements for both parts are the same.

Follow the arrows marked at the edges of one graph part to find the four center squares. Mark the 4 center meshes of each piece of canvas to correspond to the four center squares on the graph part. From the center points, count outward and lightly mark the left, right, top, and bottom edges of the design on each piece of canvas.

You are now ready to begin stitching. Stitch the design from one graph part on the first piece of canvas. Stitch the design from the other graph part on the second piece of canvas. Stitch both parts in Continental or Basketweave stitch. You have now completed the front and back of the glasses case.

## Color Key

Thread numbers refer to DMC pearl cotton. See Plate 9.

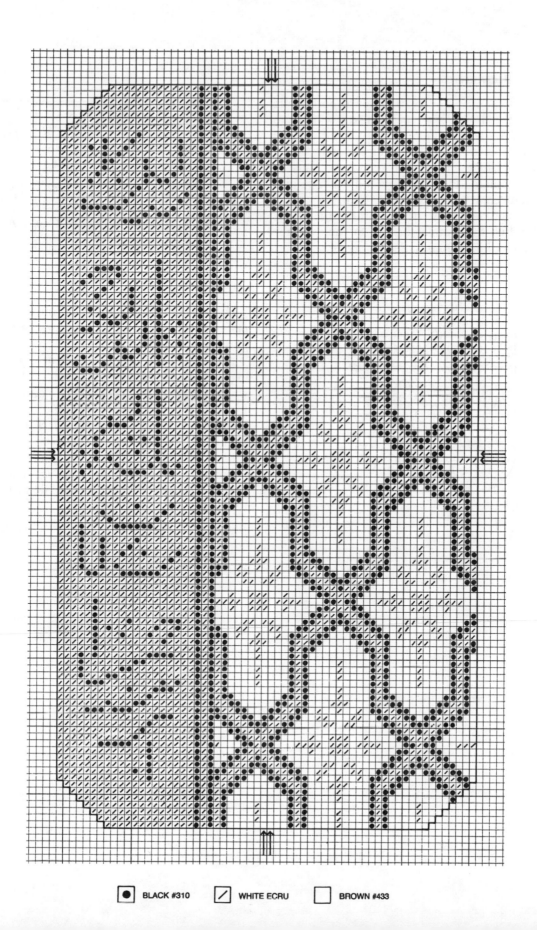

● BLACK #310    ⁄ WHITE ECRU    ☐ BROWN #433

## Creative Alternatives

DESIGN CHANGES: The black, brown, and white portion of the design is a repeat pattern which can be enlarged by adding more motifs. Therefore you can use the design to make a purse similar to the Mongol and Chinese purses. To keep the balance of the design, enlarge the black and white script area so that it occupies approximately ¼ to ⅓ of the finished design. For purse handles, stitch the repeat design on two tops similar in size to those of the Mongol and Chinese purses. See Figure 14.

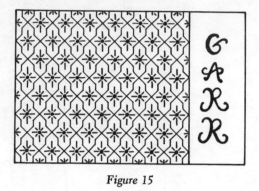

*Figure 15*

*Figure 14*

If you omit the script, you can add initials in place of the script on the glasses case or on the purse.

The design can also be used for a pillow by adding motifs. Again, keep the area of the black and white script in proportion to the repeat pattern. See Figure 15.

COLOR CHANGES: Keep the black and white but substitute for the brown a color such as green (✳3347 DMC pearl cotton) or rust (✳918).

STITCH CHANGES: The design is sufficiently busy that decorative stitches would detract from the repeat pattern.

*Kazak Rug*

Plate 1

Plate 2    Korean Cranes Pillow          Korean Pincushion          North Persian Earthenware Pillow

Chinese Cloisonné Pincushion

Plate 3    Japanese Eagle Pillow                                        Eastern Persian Lions Pillow

*Japanese Imari Pillow*

Plate 4

*Plate 5*                    *Chinese Rose Medallion Pillow*

*Persian Rose and Nightingale Pillow*                    Plate 6

*Plate 7*    *Chinese Garden Bell Pull*        *Chinese Butterflies Bell Pull*

Chinese Purse                                        Mongol Purse                    Plate 8

Turkish Glasses Case        Persian Glasses Case        Indian Glasses Case        Plate 9

Plate 10

Tibetan Purse

# PERSIAN FALCONER PILLOW

## History

The design for this pillow was freely adapted from a detail of a Persian miniature painted in Tabriz in the first half of the sixteenth century. Tabriz had long been renowned for its royal library, with its collection of miniatures, and for its large number of talented artisans and painters. In the early sixteenth century, Tabriz became the royal capital of a unified Persia under the Safavid rulers (1502–1736). Their patronage of miniature painting brought into being a number of masterpieces. When a subject for a painting was chosen, great care was taken to find the right artist, just as the right calligrapher was necessary to copy and ornament the poem which accompanied the painting.

## Canvas

The thread count for the design is 312 threads wide by 272 threads long.

If you choose 14 mesh canvas, cut and bind a piece of canvas 25½ by 22½ inches for a finished design approximately 22½ by 19½ inches.

If you choose 18 mesh canvas, cut and bind a piece of canvas 20½ by 18½ inches for a finished design approximately 17½ by 15½ inches.

## Stitching Directions

The graph is drawn in quarters—Upper Left, Upper Right, Lower Left, or Lower Right according to its position in relation to the whole design.

Follow the two arrows marked at the edges of each graph quarter until they intersect. This intersection marks the square on each quarter where you should begin stitching. Together the four squares, one from each quarter, mark the center of the design.

Find and mark the center 4 meshes of your canvas with an indelible marker to correspond to the four center squares of the graph. From these center points, count outward and lightly mark the edges of the design on the canvas.

You are now ready to begin stitching. Counting from the center outward, stitch the rider, horse, and bird, then the flowers. Stitch the gold borders and then the script and its background. Finally, fill in the light blue background.

## Color and Stitch Key

The colors are similar to those used in many Persian miniatures. Yarn numbers refer to Paternayan yarn. The various stitches used are noted on the key. See Plate 14.

*Upper Right*

| | | |
|---|---|---|
| ☒ DARK GOLD #752 | ◩ LIGHT GOLD #755 | ⊙ MEDIUM GRAY #202 |
| ◪ DARK GOLD #752 SCOTCH STITCH OVER 4 MESHES | ◣ CHARCOAL GRAY #221 | ⌊ WHITE #261 |
| ⊡ MEDIUM GOLD #754 | ◤ DARK GRAY #200 | ⊡ FLESH #875 |

| | BROWN #402 | | RED #841 | | DARK BLUE #542 |
|---|---|---|---|---|---|
| | DARK GREEN #620 | | ORANGE #800 | | MEDIUM BLUE #544 |
| | MEDIUM GREEN #621 | | PURPLE #332 | | LIGHT BLUE #505 JACQUARD STITCH VARIATION |

*Lower Right*

*Upper Left*

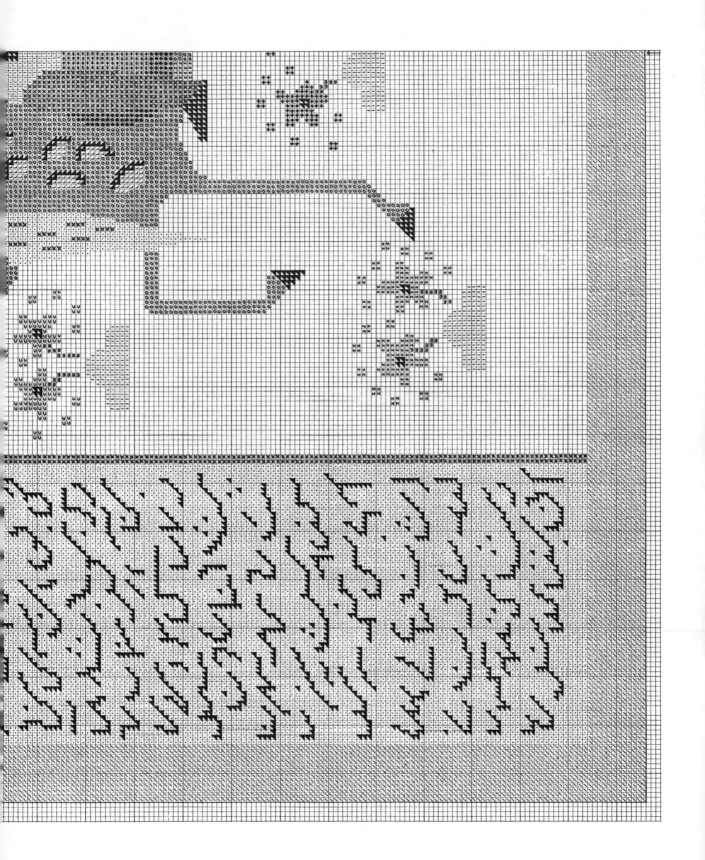

*Lower Left*

## Creative Alternatives

DESIGN CHANGES: To combine the Persian Falconer and Persian Hunter pillows into a rug, see the Creative Alternatives for the Persian Hunter pillow.

If you want to make a smaller pillow, omit the border and the areas with script.

COLOR CHANGES: See Persian Hunter pillow. If you decide to use a dark background such as dark blue or green, consider changing the color of the horse to a lighter gray.

STITCH CHANGES: See the Persian Hunter pillow.

# PERSIAN HUNTER PILLOW

## History

The design for this pillow is freely adapted from a detail of a Persian miniature painted in Shiraz in 1546. The horseman is part of a larger royal hunting party. This party became the subject of a painting for a book on the life of the ruler, Timur. The highly stylized figures and the jewel-like colors reflect the increasing refinement of Persian miniature painting in the sixteenth century under the patronage of the Safavid dynasty. These miniatures were usually commissioned to fill an album or to illustrate a manuscript. These miniatures gathered together in a single volume furnished the leaders of the time, who spent much of their lives in tents, while fighting or hunting, with portable art galleries of miniature masterpieces.

## Canvas

The thread count for the design is 312 threads wide by 272 threads long.

If you choose 14 mesh canvas, cut and bind a piece of canvas 25½ by 22½ inches for a finished design approximately 22½ by 19½ inches.

If you choose 18 mesh canvas, cut and bind a piece of canvas 20½ by 18½ inches for a finished design approximately 17½ by 15½ inches.

## Stitching Directions

The graph is drawn in quarters—Upper Left, Upper Right, Lower Left, or Lower Right according to its position in relation to the whole design.

Follow the two arrows marked at the edges of each graph quarter until they intersect. This intersection marks the square on each quarter where you should begin stitching. Together, the four squares, one from each quarter, mark the center of the design.

Find and mark the center 4 meshes of your canvas with an indelible marker to correspond to the four center squares of the graph. From these center points, count outward and lightly mark the edges of the design on the canvas.

You are now ready to begin stitching. Counting from the center outward, stitch the rider, horse, and cat, then the flowers. Stitch the gold borders and then the lettering and its background. Finally, fill in the light blue background.

## Color and Stitch Key

The colors are similar to those used in many Persian miniatures. Yarn numbers refer to Paternayan yarn. The various stitches used are noted on the key. See Plate 14.

*Upper Right*

| | | | |
|---|---|---|---|
| ☒ DARK GOLD #752 | ◹ LIGHT GOLD #755 | ◯ MEDIUM GRAY #202 | |
| ◿ DARK GOLD #752 SCOTCH STITCH OVER 4 MESHES | ◣ CHARCOAL GRAY #221 | ═ LIGHT GRAY #203 | |
| ⦁ MEDIUM GOLD #754 | ◥ DARK GRAY #200 | ⦂ FLESH #875 | |

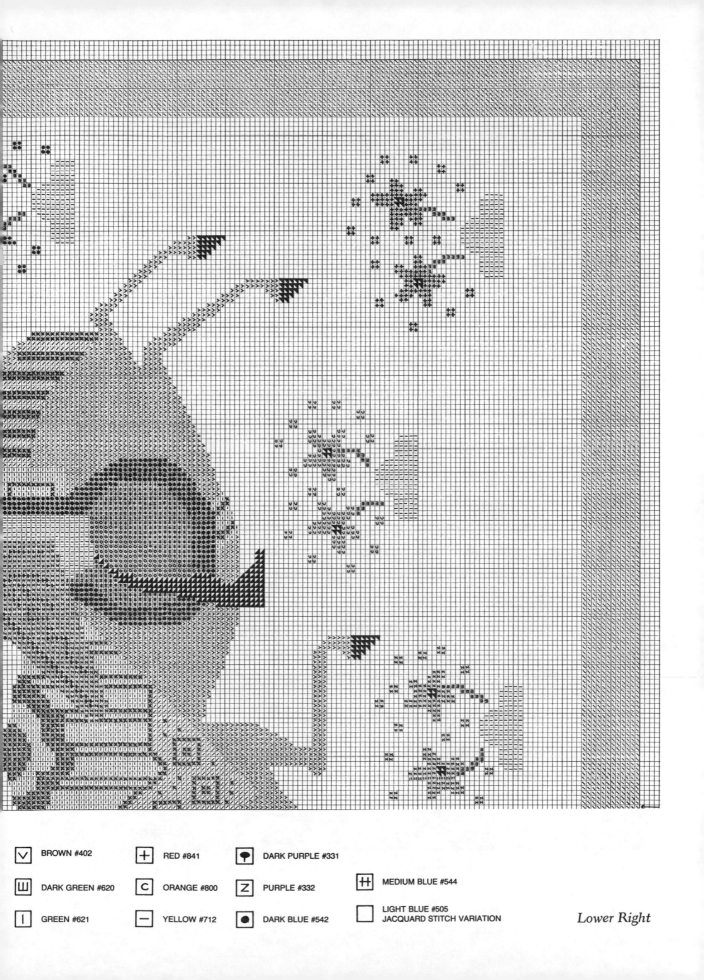

| | | |
|---|---|---|
| ⋁ BROWN #402 | ✚ RED #841 | ⬤ DARK PURPLE #331 |
| Ш DARK GREEN #620 | C ORANGE #800 | Z PURPLE #332 | ⊞ MEDIUM BLUE #544 |
| I GREEN #621 | — YELLOW #712 | ⬤ DARK BLUE #542 | LIGHT BLUE #505 JACQUARD STITCH VARIATION |

*Lower Right*

*Upper Left*

*Lower Left*

## Creative Alternatives

DESIGN CHANGES: You can combine the Persian Falconer and Persian Hunter pillows together to make a rug by the following procedure: You will treat the eight parts of the two graphs as one design with the Persian Falconer on top of the Persian Hunter. Omit all border areas so that you can join the two pillows into one design. Replace all script areas with light blue background. Now readjust the flower units, sprinkling them to cover the background evenly. Add several flower units to fill in the areas that once contained script. Stitch the background in Basketweave stitch. Add a gold border around the two designs. Stitch the rug on 10 mesh canvas. See Figure 16.

COLOR CHANGES: Many colors other than light blue will work well for the background, such as white and light green. If you use light green, check that there is sufficient contrast between the background and the green flower mounds and stems. You may want to change the latter to a darker green.

A dark background instead of a pale one will make the other colors appear jewel-bright. If you de-

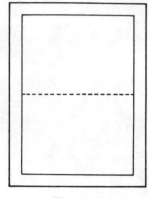

*Figure 16*

cide to use a dark color, such as dark blue or green, check that the horse's black mane, tail, and hooves will not be lost. You may also want to make the horse a lighter brown and the cat a lighter gray.

STITCH CHANGES: Most diagonal stitches will work well as a background. If you want to change stitches, try Milanese or Oriental stitch. If you change the border from Scotch stitch to rows of Slanting Gobelin stitch, then you can use Scotch stitch as a background.

# PERSIAN RUG

## History

This rug is adapted from a carpet designed by an artist under the Safavid dynasty of Persia. Safavid carpets were of a higher quality than the ordinary rugs made by nomads and villagers. As works of art, they were often, as here, enlarged versions of Persian miniature paintings. Although Persia had been invaded by the armies of Islam in the seventh century, the Persians were not conquered by Arab culture. They kept their own language although they wrote it in Arabic characters. As the stronghold of the minority Islamic Shi'ite sect, the Persians were not as strict as the adherents of the Sunnite doctrine, which largely forbade representations of living things. Persian carpets often portray animals, plants, and human beings, as in this example from the eighteenth century.

## Canvas

The thread count for the rug is 446 threads wide by 682 threads long.

If you choose 10 mesh canvas, cut and bind a piece of canvas 47½ by 71½ inches for a finished design approximately 44½ by 68½ inches in size.

If you choose 12 mesh canvas, cut and bind a piece of canvas 40½ by 60 inches for a finished design approximately 37½ by 57 inches.

## Stitching Directions

The rug graph is drawn in ten parts—Graphs A, B, C, D, E, F, G, H, I, and J. Eight parts represent the field of the rug. Two parts together represent the lower right quarter of the border. Figure 17 demonstrates how the ten parts of the rug graph fit together.

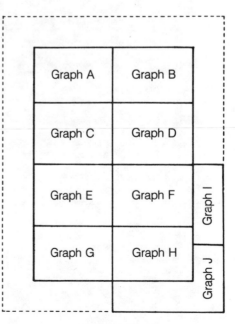

*Figure 17*

Persian Rug

Follow the arrows marked at the edges of the eight field graph parts until the arrow lines intersect. These four squares on Graphs C, D, E, and F, mark the center of the design.

Find and mark the center 4 meshes of your canvas with an indelible marker to correspond to the four center squares of the graph parts. From these meshes, count 223 threads to the left, 223 threads to the right, 341 threads to the top, and 341 threads to the bottom and mark these points, which are the edges of the design.

You are now ready to begin stitching. Counting from the center, stitch Graphs C, D, E, and F. Then stitch Graphs A, B, G, and H in their appropriate places as shown in Figure 17.

Stitch Graphs I and J of the lower right quarter of the border, fitting them along the lower right quarter of the rug field. Stitch the lower left quarter of the border in a mirror image of the lower right quarter. You will now have completed the lower half of the border. Stitch the upper half of the border in a mirror image of the lower half.

Stitch the entire design in Continental or Basketweave stitch.

## Color Key

The background of the original rug was black and the other colors were more intense. I changed the background to brown and chose softer colors. Yarn numbers refer to Paternayan yarns. See Plate 15.

## Creative Alternatives

DESIGN CHANGES: A number of the design details, alone or in combination, can be used for pillows or pincushions. The elephant, driver, and rider would make a pillow, as would the peacock, horse and rider, or the birds. The dog motif would also be appropriate for pincushions. Stitch these motifs on 14 or 18 mesh canvas and add a sprinkling of flower motifs.

COLOR CHANGES: For a light brown background, reverse the dark brown and light brown on the color key. For a white background, change the color key as follows: dark brown to white, light brown to dark brown, white to light brown. All other colors remain the same.

The rug would also be attractive with a dark gray background. Change the color key as follows: dark brown to dark gray ($\divideontimes$200 Paternayan yarn), medium brown to medium gray ($\divideontimes$202), light brown to light gray ($\divideontimes$203). If you use gray, retain the light brown for the men's faces.

STITCH CHANGES: For best wear, a rug should be stitched in Continental or Basketweave stitch. Most decorative stitches carry a thread over 2 or more meshes. The longer the thread, the more easily it will wear. If you use any of the motifs for a pillow or a pincushion, you can then experiment with decorative stitches.

| ⬤ | CHARCOAL GRAY #221 | — | MEDIUM BROWN #463 |
|---|---|---|---|
| ☐ | DARK BROWN #462 | ╱ | LIGHT BROWN #465 |

*Graph A*

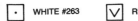
*Graph B*

*Graph C*

*Graph D*

*Graph E*

*Graph F*

*Graph G*

*Graph H*

*Graph I*

Graph J

*East Persian Lions Pillow*

# EAST PERSIAN LIONS PILLOW

## History

The design for this pillow is adapted from a detail taken from an East Persian shroud dating from about the eighth or ninth century A.D. The shroud, used as a winding sheet for burying the dead, consists of a series of roundels, each depicting two mythical-looking lions confronting one another. Highly stylized lions in potential combat were a common theme on Persian fabrics. They appear both in semimythical form and in realistic representation on some of the more famous hunting carpets. The bold and somewhat jagged pattern of this design reflects not only the influence of Islam but an earlier indigenous Near Eastern affinity for powerful stylization emphasizing abstraction, ornamentation, and geometric forms.

## Canvas

The thread count for the design is 276 threads wide by 256 threads long.

If you choose 14 mesh canvas, cut and bind a piece of canvas 23 by 21½ inches for a finished design approximately 20 by 18½ inches.

If you choose 18 mesh canvas, cut and bind a piece of canvas 18½ by 17½ inches for a finished design approximately 15½ by 14½ inches.

## Stitching Directions

The graph is drawn in two parts—Upper Right and Lower Right. Together these two parts represent the right half of the finished design.

Follow the arrows marked at the edges of each graph part until they intersect. These two intersections correspond to the center of your canvas and are the points where you will begin stitching.

Mark the center of your canvas with an indelible marker to correspond to the two graph intersection squares. Counting from these squares, mark the top, bottom, and right edges of the design on your canvas. The number of threads from the top edge to the bottom edge of the design should be 256, the vertical thread count; the number of threads from the center to the right edge should be 138, half the horizontal thread count.

You are now ready to begin stitching. Starting at the center of your canvas, stitch the black and

*Upper Right*

white portions of the graph marked Upper Right, then the black and white portions of the graph marked Lower Right. You will now have completed the black and white parts of half the design. Stitch the black and white parts of the left half of the design in a mirror image to the right half. Finally, fill in the dark orange and orange background.

## Color and Stitch Key

The colors are similar to those in the original shroud. Thread numbers refer to DMC pearl cotton. The location of the stitches used is listed on the key. The key instructs you to stitch St. George and St. Andrew Cross stitch in dark orange and orange. Referring to the stitch diagrams for St. George and St. Andrew Cross stitch, work step 1 in dark orange and step 2 in orange. See Plate 3.

## Creative Alternatives

DESIGN CHANGES: For a smaller pillow, stitch the two lions, omitting the border.

For another pillow, stitch only one lion. Around it stitch a square border of black Slanting Gobelin stitch and then a 16-row border of white Scotch stitch.

COLOR CHANGES: Keep the black as it is and reverse the orange and white so that the lions and details are orange and the background is white.

Or keep the orange as it is and reverse the black and white so that the lions are black and the outlines and details are white.

Or keep the black and white design and stitch a two-tone green background (✳368 and ✳320 DMC pearl cotton) or a two-tone blue background (✳827 and ✳826).

STITCH CHANGES: Try Woven stitch variation or a two-tone Double Cross stitch for the background.

# INDIAN YANTRA PILLOW

## History

This design is adapted from a Jain diagram of the cosmos from Rajasthan, India, in the late eighteenth century. The Jain yantra, as such diagrams were often known, is painted with gouache on cloth. The function of the yantra, as part of the cult of Tantra in India, is to represent symbolically the process of the creation of space-time and the objective universe. The yantra focuses the imagination and emotion of the meditating believer on phases of genesis in time which ultimately find their ground in the goddess of creation. Buddhist, Hindu, and Jain adherents each practice Tantra in their own way, but all use yantras in one form or another as an aid to meditation.

## Canvas

The thread count for the design is 248 threads square.

If you choose 14 mesh canvas, cut and bind a piece of canvas 21 inches square for a finished design approximately 18 inches square.

If you choose 18 mesh canvas, cut and bind a piece of canvas 17 inches square for a finished design approximately 14 inches square.

## Stitching Directions

The graph is drawn in quarters—Upper Left, Upper Right, Lower Left, or Lower Right according to its position in relation to the whole design.

Follow the two arrows marked at the border of each graph quarter until they intersect. This intersection marks the square on each quarter where you should begin stitching. Together, the four squares, one from each quarter, mark the center of the design.

Find and mark the center 4 meshes of your canvas with an indelible marker to correspond to the four center squares of the graph. From these center points, count outward and lightly mark the edges of the design on the canvas.

You are now ready to begin stitching. Counting from the center outward, stitch first the charcoal gray and red outlines. Then fill in the various colors, and finally, stitch the background.

## Color and Stitch Key

The colors used are approximately those of the original painting. Yarn numbers refer to Paternayan yarn. The various decorative stitches and their locations are noted on the key. See Plate 18.

| | CHARCOAL GRAY #221 | | GREEN #652 |
|---|---|---|---|
| X | RED #841 | + | GREEN #652 DOUBLE CROSS STITCH |
| Z | RED #841 SLANTING GOBELIN STITCH | | GREEN #652 SLANTING GOBELIN STITCH |
| ● | RED #841 ST. GEORGE AND ST. ANDREW CROSS STITCH | H | LIGHT GREEN #653 SLANTING GOBELIN STITCH |

| | YELLOW #713 MILANESE STITCH | | | LIGHT RED #875 | | | |
| | YELLOW #713 DIAGONAL MOSAIC STITCH | | | LIGHT RED #875 DIAGONAL SCOTCH STITCH | | | LIGHT BLUE #505 SLANTING GOBELIN STITCH |
| | YELLOW #713 SLANTING GOBELIN STITCH | | | LIGHT RED #875 SLANTING GOBELIN STITCH | | | CAMEL #443 |
| | WHITE #260 SLANTING GOBELIN STITCH | | | LIGHT BLUE #505 | | | CAMEL #443 WOVEN STITCH |

*Upper Right*

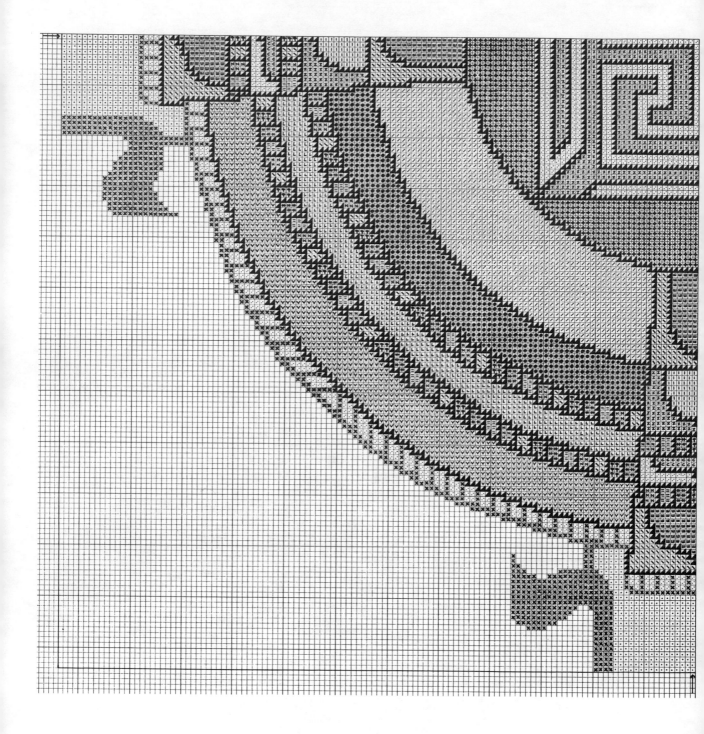

*Lower Left*

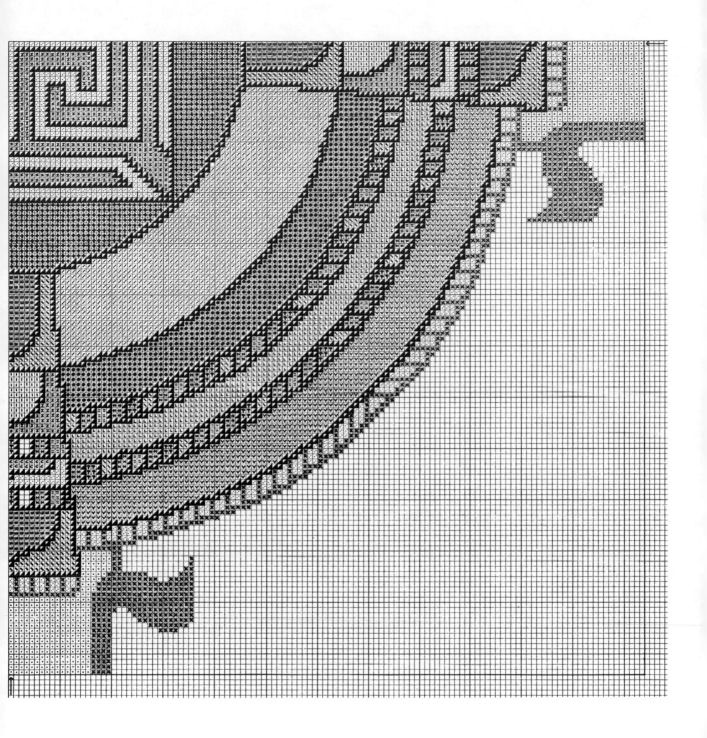

*Lower Right*

## Creative Alternatives

DESIGN CHANGES: Make a round pillow by ending the design with the circular red outline. To make a rug, use three of the design squares together on 10 mesh canvas. Plan a red border around each of the design squares. See Figure 18.

COLOR CHANGES: Substitute white for all yellow areas, and red for all blue and green areas. Keep all other colors as they are charted. The pillow will be predominantly red, white, and camel in color.

For another color combination use four values of blue (✕500, ✕502, ✕504, and ✕506 Paternayan yarn) plus white. Use navy or the darkest blue in the yarn series you choose for outlines.

STITCH CHANGES: If you decide to make a rug by combining three design squares together, stitch the whole rug in Basketweave or Continental.

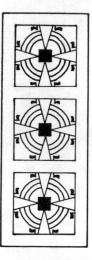

*Figure 18*

# INDIAN ASTRONOMICAL CHART PILLOW

## History

The design for this pillow is adapted from an eighteenth-century ink and color painting from Himachal Pradesh, in India. The design served both as a means for computing astronomical periods and as a yantra aiding meditation. The concept of creation and space-time lies at the heart of the cult of Tantra in India. Tantric diagrams summarize in various forms the cosmic designs of the universe in space and time. Since astrology calculated the fate of the individual and explained which actions to take, the believers in Tantra made much use of astrological horoscopes. This required numerous observations of the heavens and many diagrams of the varying relations of constellations, planets, lunar phases, and so on, to world time. All such charts, as symbolic insights into the genesis of creation and space-time, functioned also as yantras for meditation.

## Canvas

The thread count for the design is 184 threads square.

If you choose 12 mesh canvas, cut and bind a piece of canvas 18½ inches square for a finished design approximately 15½ inches square.

If you choose 14 mesh canvas, cut and bind a piece of canvas 16 inches square for a finished design approximately 13 inches square.

Using 18 mesh canvas, cut and bind a piece of canvas 13½ inches square for a finished design approximately 10½ inches square.

## Stitching Directions

The graph is drawn in halves—Left Half and Right Half. Follow the four arrows marked at the edges of each graph half until they intersect. These four intersection squares, two on each graph half, are the center of the design and mark the points where you should begin stitching.

Find and mark the center 4 meshes of your canvas with an indelible marker so that they correspond to the four center squares on the graph halves. From these center points, count outward and lightly mark the edges of the design on the canvas.

You are now ready to begin stitching. Counting from the center points outward, first stitch the charcoal gray Continental stitch, Cross stitch, and Diagonal Mosaic stitch outlines, then fill in the decorative stitches and colors, and finally stitch the background.

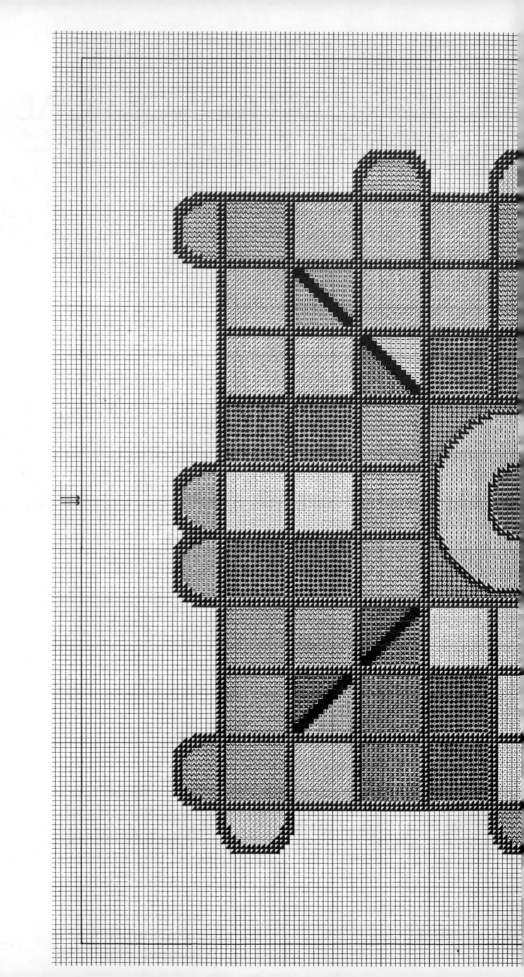

*Left Half*

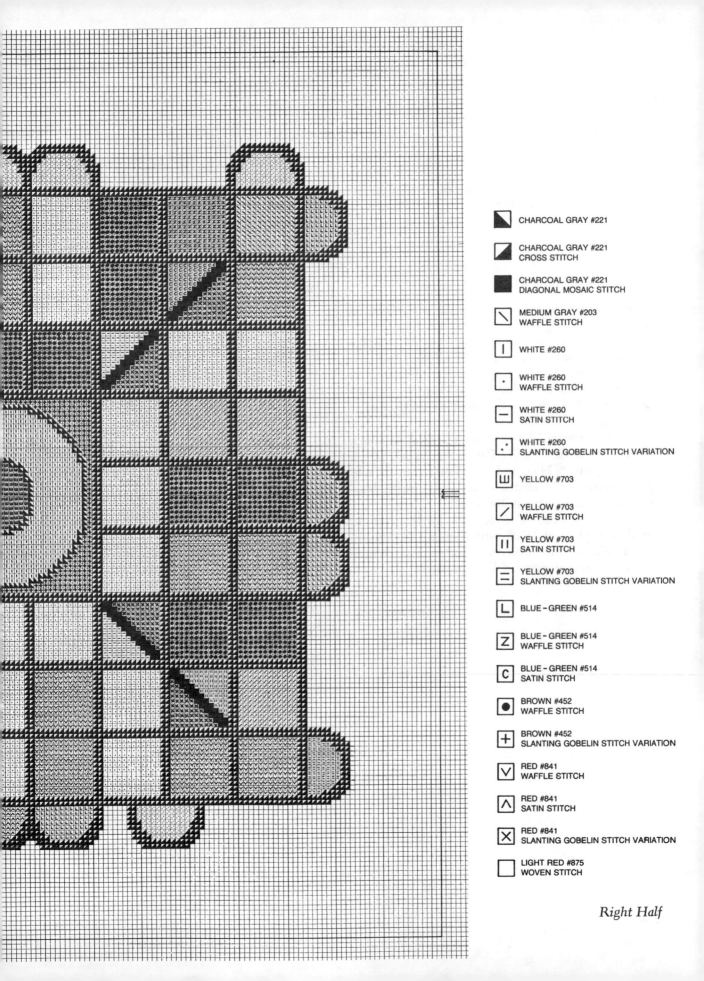

CHARCOAL GRAY #221

CHARCOAL GRAY #221
CROSS STITCH

CHARCOAL GRAY #221
DIAGONAL MOSAIC STITCH

MEDIUM GRAY #203
WAFFLE STITCH

WHITE #260

WHITE #260
WAFFLE STITCH

WHITE #260
SATIN STITCH

WHITE #260
SLANTING GOBELIN STITCH VARIATION

YELLOW #703

YELLOW #703
WAFFLE STITCH

YELLOW #703
SATIN STITCH

YELLOW #703
SLANTING GOBELIN STITCH VARIATION

BLUE – GREEN #514

BLUE – GREEN #514
WAFFLE STITCH

BLUE – GREEN #514
SATIN STITCH

BROWN #452
WAFFLE STITCH

BROWN #452
SLANTING GOBELIN STITCH VARIATION

RED #841
WAFFLE STITCH

RED #841
SATIN STITCH

RED #841
SLANTING GOBELIN STITCH VARIATION

LIGHT RED #875
WOVEN STITCH

*Right Half*

## Color and Stitch Key

The yarn colors listed are similar to those of the original design. Yarn numbers refer to Paternayan yarn. The location of the various stitches is indicated on the key. See Plate 18.

## Creative Alternatives

DESIGN CHANGES: To make a rug, use six of the pillow designs together on 10 mesh canvas. Plan a narrow charcoal gray border around each design unit as in Figure 19; or omit the border around each unit, replacing it with a border around the rug as in Figure 20. Vary the color combinations from chart to chart so that the arrangement of each chart is different.

COLOR CHANGES: For a softer color combination, change red to rust (✳872 Paternayan yarn), yellow to light gold (✳743), and the background to light gray (✳204). The charcoal gray, gray, white, blue-green, and brown remain the same.

STITCH CHANGES: Use Rhodes stitch over 12 meshes in place of Waffle stitch or use the squares to experiment with different stitches. Use Woven stitch variation in place of Woven stitch.

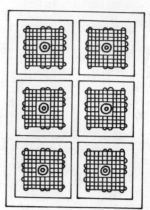

*Figure 19*

**Figure 20**

# INDIAN EGG PILLOW

## History

The design for this pillow is adapted from an eighteenth-century gouache on paper painting from Rajasthan, India. In the cult of Tantra, this diagram symbolizes the fertilized world egg (the beige circle in the center of the field of red) as it divides into regions and currents of energy represented by the various panels of color on both sides of the egg. This is part of the Tantric theory of the genesis of the world from the original unity symbolized by an egg. The powerful goddess of creation conceives of man, which makes possible the fertilized egg. This marks the beginning of the process of the creation of space-time, energy, and the objective universe. The Tantric belief in the essential position of woman as the universal mover and ultimate creator of the universe is in sharp contrast to patriarchal, religious concepts of the origin of the world dominating most ideologies to the west of India.

## Canvas

The thread count for the pillow is 240 threads wide by 152 threads long.

If you choose 12 mesh canvas, cut and bind a piece of canvas 23 by 15½ inches for a finished design approximately 20 by 12½ inches.

If you choose 14 mesh canvas, cut and bind a piece of canvas 20 by 14 inches for a finished design approximately 17 by 11 inches.

Using 18 mesh canvas, cut and bind a piece of canvas 16½ by 11½ inches for a finished design approximately 13½ by 8½ inches.

## Stitching Directions

The graph is drawn in halves—Left Half and Right Half. Follow the four arrows marked at the edges of each graph half until they intersect. These four intersection squares, two on each graph half, are the center of the design and mark the points where you should begin stitching.

Find and mark the center 4 meshes of your canvas with an indelible marker so that they correspond to the four center squares on the graph halves. From these center points, count outward and lightly mark the edges of the design on the canvas.

You are now ready to begin stitching. Counting from the center points outward, first stitch the charcoal gray Continental stitch and Slanting Gobelin stitch outlines, then fill in the decorative stitches and colors, and finally stitch the background.

## Color and Stitch Key

The yarn colors in the color key are close to those in the original Tantric painting. Yarn numbers refer to Paternayan yarn. The location of the various stitches is indicated on the key. See Plate 18.

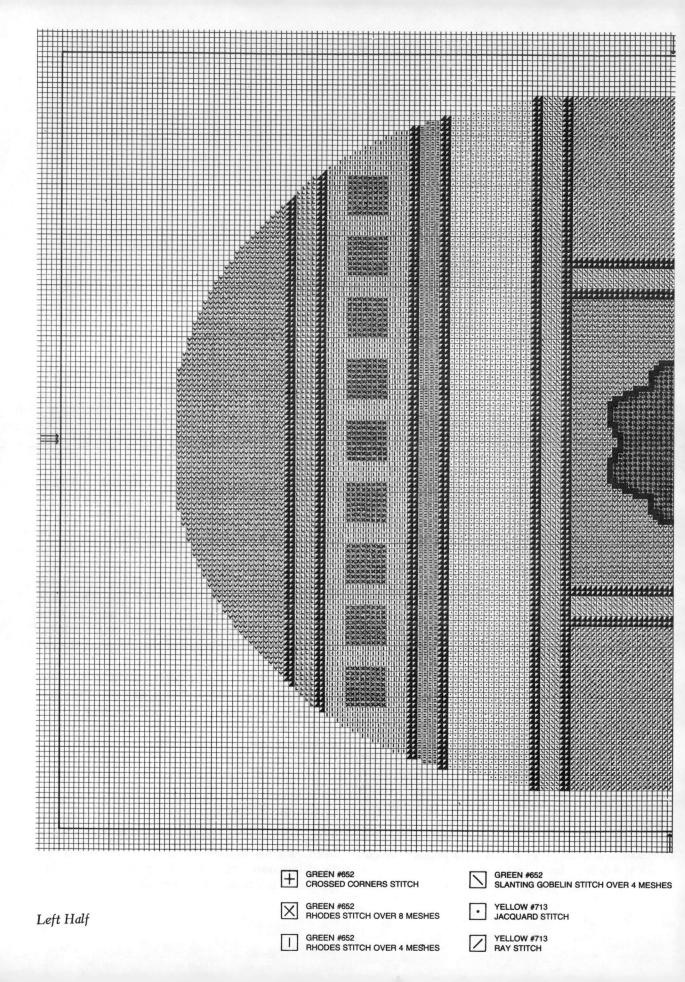

*Left Half*

| | GREEN #652<br>CROSSED CORNERS STITCH | | GREEN #652<br>SLANTING GOBELIN STITCH OVER 4 MESHES |
| | GREEN #652<br>RHODES STITCH OVER 8 MESHES | | YELLOW #713<br>JACQUARD STITCH |
| | GREEN #652<br>RHODES STITCH OVER 4 MESHES | | YELLOW #713<br>RAY STITCH |

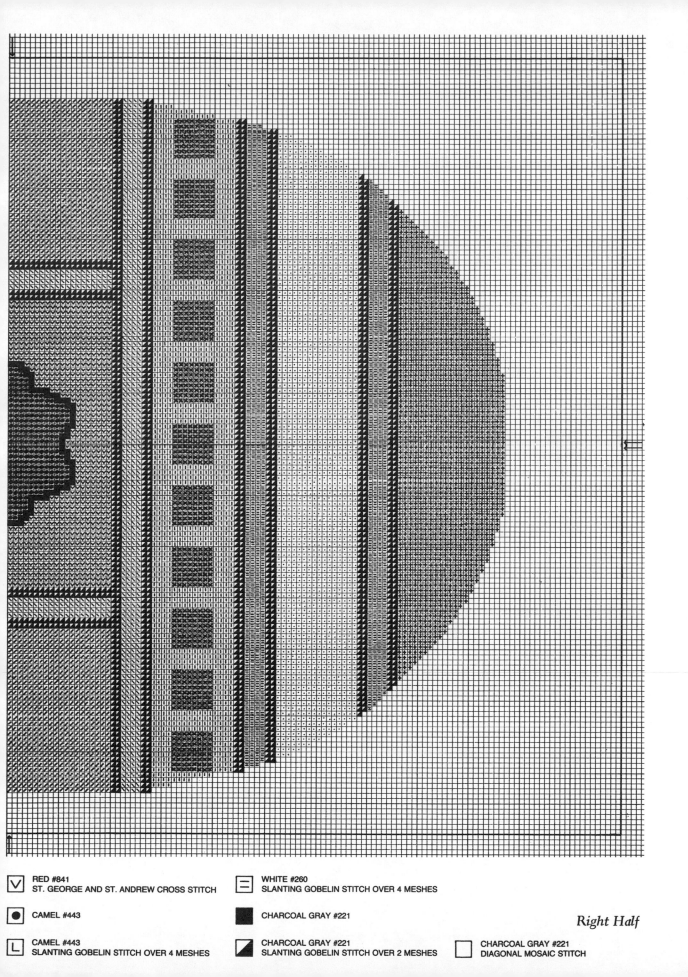

*Right Half*

| | RED #841 ST. GEORGE AND ST. ANDREW CROSS STITCH | | WHITE #260 SLANTING GOBELIN STITCH OVER 4 MESHES |
| --- | --- | --- | --- |
| | CAMEL #443 | | CHARCOAL GRAY #221 |
| | CAMEL #443 SLANTING GOBELIN STITCH OVER 4 MESHES | | CHARCOAL GRAY #221 SLANTING GOBELIN STITCH OVER 2 MESHES |
| | | | CHARCOAL GRAY #221 DIAGONAL MOSAIC STITCH |

## Creative Alternatives

DESIGN AND STITCH CHANGES: The egg pillow is intended as a sampler. Adding a border of red, charcoal gray, yellow, and green around the design will give areas for 4 additional stitches. Construct the border as follows: 4-stitch red border, 2-stitch charcoal border, 8-stitch yellow border, 2-stitch charcoal border, 12-stitch green border. See Figure 21. Use Crossed Corners stitch for the red border, Cross stitch for both charcoal borders, Fern stitch for the yellow border, and Milanese or Oriental stitch for the green border.

Several of the stitches used in the egg pattern are repeated: the Rhodes stitch and Ray stitch, for example, are used in two areas. Instead of repeating these stitches, use another stitch for the second area, such as the Rhodes stitch in one area and the Tile stitch in another.

COLOR CHANGES: The colors of the original egg design are bright and are made even more intense

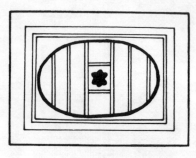

*Figure 21*

by the dark background. For a different effect, try a light background in place of the charcoal gray.

Change the colors to charcoal gray outlines, dark red (✳930 Paternayan yarn), the same green, light gold (✳734), and off-white (✳262) for a softer color combination.

# INDIAN GLASSES CASE

## History

The design of this glasses case is adapted from the upper border of a wall painting of a boar hunt in Lepakshi temple near Hindupur in South India dating from about 1540. If this design seems to be a more flowery representation of the abstract design of the Persian glasses case, there is good reason for the close resemblance. Indian art often intermixed with that of Persia and both were subject to the influence of Islam through the frequent inroads of its armies. Nonetheless, the influence of the classical and indigenous South Indian culture is also apparent in the more fluid and softer lines, muted colors, and closer links to naturalism of this design, which lacks that emphasis on geometric design found in even the most arabesque of Persian designs.

## Canvas

The thread count for the design is 66 threads by 110 threads.

Cut and bind two pieces of 18 mesh canvas 6½ by 9½ inches for a finished design approximately 3½ by 6½ inches.

## Stitching Directions

Follow the arrows marked at the edges of the graph to find the four center squares. Mark the 4 center meshes of each piece of canvas with an indelible marker to correspond to the four center squares on the graph. From the center points, count outward and lightly mark the left, right, top, and bottom edges of the design on each piece of canvas.

You are now ready to begin stitching. Counting from the center points, stitch the design on one piece of canvas. Repeat the design on the second piece of canvas. Stitch both parts in Continental or Basketweave stitch. You have now completed the front and back of the glasses case.

## Color Key

The colors are approximately those of the original border design. Thread numbers refer to DMC pearl cotton. See Plate 9.

93

## Creative Alternatives

DESIGN CHANGES: This design will work well as a purse similar to the Mongol and Chinese purses. Use 14 or 18 mesh canvas. Omitting the black, brown, and beige stripes at the edges of the glasses case, stitch three panels of the design side by side so that the half circles are joined into whole circles. Now add a black, brown, and beige striped border around the design. Keep adding rows to the border until the purse reaches the size you want. Stitch two tops of black, brown, and beige stripes to use as handles. See Figure 22. Also see Mongol and Chinese purses.

Figure 23

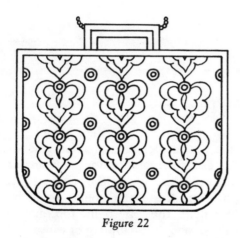

Figure 22

This design can also be used for a bell pull on 10 mesh canvas. Omitting the border, stitch the design motifs, one below another, until the bell pull reaches the approximate length you want. Now stitch a black, brown, and beige border around the whole bell pull. Add several rows to the border if you want to increase the width of the bell pull. See Figure 23. Trim with a tassel. See instructions for tassels.

COLOR CHANGES: Use the original colors but change their order. Keep the black and brown as used but switch the order of the blue-green and beige so that the beige areas on the original are now blue-green and the blue-green areas on the original are now beige. Any number of color combinations can be used in one of these two ways. Preserving the black, brown, and beige, you might use rust (⁂918 DMC pearl cotton), orange (⁂435), gold (⁂783), or green (⁂368) as a fourth color in place of the blue-green.

STITCH CHANGES: Large-scale decorative stitches will not work well for this design because of the lack of large spaces. You might try Mosaic stitch, Diagonal Mosaic stitch, or Cross stitch for the background. The one place that has room for a decorative stitch is the beige border, but I do not recommend that you use a pattern stitch here. The design is sufficiently busy that the addition of texture other than a simple background stitch will detract from it.

● BLACK #310    Ⅴ BROWN #433    · BEIGE #644    ☐ BLUE-GREEN #502

*Tibetan Purse*

# TIBETAN PURSE

## History

The design for this purse is adapted from an early nineteenth-century Tibetan saddle rug. These rugs were not cushions intended for sitting but ornamental coverings (caparisons) to fit under the saddle to prevent it from chafing the horse's back. Like the original Tibetan saddle rug, the purse has at its center the Chinese character shou, meaning long life. This shou medallion is unusual because it reproduces the complete shou rather than merely doubling the lower half, as was more common. Below the shou are abstract representations of half-dragons or of Sanskrit gnomes. The two brown cruciform squares above the shou mark the spots where this saddle rug was attached beneath the saddle. The small cones on the outer border are symbols for the stupas or domes of Lamaist temples.

The Tibetan purse can be made in two ways. The first, shown in the photograph, uses bone handles for which you stitch the purse body and gusset. The second way uses the purse body and a top similar to those of the Mongol and Chinese purses.

The bone handles, such as the ones used in the model, are two straight bars of pierced bone measuring approximately the width of the finished purse. These handles were used on purses made in China for export to the United States between the two world wars and can be found quite frequently in antique shops.

The graph for the purse is drawn in three parts— Graphs A, B, and C. Graph A represents the right half of the purse body. Graph B is the purse gusset (used only in Method 1). Graph C is the purse top (used only in Method 2).

## METHOD 1

Method 1 uses the purse body, gusset, and bone handles for a finished purse resembling the model in the photograph.

### Canvas

The thread count for the purse body is 144 threads wide by 168 threads long. The gusset for the purse is a separate piece of canvas measuring 22 threads wide by 406 threads long.

Using 18 mesh canvas, cut and bind two pieces of canvas each 11 by 12½ inches for finished designs approximately 8 by 9½ inches. Also cut and bind a piece of canvas 4 by 25½ inches for a finished gusset approximately 1 by 22½ inches.

## Stitching Directions

THE PURSE BODY: Graph A represents the right half of the purse body. Follow the arrows marked at the edges of Graph A until they intersect. These two intersection squares correspond to the center of the canvas and are the points where you will begin stitching.

Mark the center of your first piece of canvas with an indelible marker to correspond to the two graph intersection squares. Counting from these canvas meshes, mark the right, top, and bottom edges of the design on your canvas. Mark the center meshes and the right, top, and bottom edges of the design on your second piece of canvas so that it is identical to the first.

You are now ready to begin stitching. Stitch the first piece of canvas. Counting from the center points, stitch all design parts of Graph A except the Diagonal Mosaic stitch background. Stitch the design for the left half in a mirror image of the right half. Now fill in the background.

Stitch the second piece of canvas as you stitched the first piece. You have now completed the two pieces of the purse body.

THE PURSE GUSSET: Mark the center of the gusset strip of canvas with an indelible marker. Counting from the center, mark the edges of the design so that the length of the gusset is 406 threads and the width is 22 threads.

Starting at one end of the gusset, stitch the first 2 rows above arrow A. Then stitch the rows marked A through B. Repeat the rows marked A through B twenty-four times for a total of twenty-five units. Stitch the last 4 rows.

Because your stitching tension dictates the exact measurement of a strip of finished needlepoint, check the length of the gusset against the purse body. The gusset should fit around three sides of the body, ending approximately 1 inch below the top edge. See Figure 24. If the gusset is a bit short, add a few rows to each end until it is the proper length.

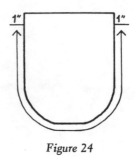

*Figure 24*

## Color and Stitch Key

The colors in the color key are close to those of the rug from which the purse was adapted. The numbers refer to DMC pearl cotton. The location and choice of stitches are indicated on the key. See Plate 10.

## Finishing

Finishing instructions for the Tibetan purse are under the section called Finishing (Purse with Bone Handles).

*Figure 25*

## METHOD 2

Method 2 uses the purse body and top for a finished purse similar to the Mongol and Chinese purses.

## Canvas

The thread count for the purse body is 144 threads wide by 168 threads long. The purse top is a separate piece for which the thread count is 58 threads wide by 50 threads long.

If you choose 14 mesh canvas, cut and bind two pieces of canvas 13½ by 15 inches for finished designs approximately 10½ by 12 inches. Also cut and bind two pieces of canvas for the top 7 by 6½ inches for finished designs 4 by 3½ inches.

If you choose 18 mesh canvas, cut and bind two pieces of canvas 11 by 12½ inches for finished designs approximately 8 by 9½ inches. Also cut and bind two pieces of canvas for the top 6 by 5½ inches for finished designs 3 by 2½ inches.

## Stitching Directions

THE PURSE BODY: Mark the canvas and stitch the two sides of the purse body according to the instructions in Method 1.

THE PURSE TOP: Follow the arrows marked at the edges of Graph C to find the four center squares. Mark, with an indelible marker, the 4 center meshes of one piece of canvas to correspond to the four center squares on the graph. From the center points, count outward and lightly mark the left, right, top, and bottom edges of the design on the canvas.

Mark the center meshes and design edges on a second piece of canvas so that it is identical to the first.

Counting from the center points, stitch Graph C. Repeat Graph C on your second piece of canvas.

## Color and Stitch Key

Follow the color and stitch key instructions used in Method 1.

## Finishing

Finish the purse referring to the finishing instructions for Purse with Needlepoint Top.

## Creative Alternatives

DESIGN CHANGES: Make a pillow of the purse by changing the border to a rectangle. Stitch the center medallion. Stitch the brown and red section at the upper part of the purse on the upper and lower parts of the pillow. Stitch the brown and blue-green notches at the upper part of the purse on the upper and lower parts of the pillow. See Figure 25.

COLOR CHANGES: Try the following color combination: change dark blue-green to dark brown (✳938 DMC pearl cotton), light blue-green to light brown (✳644), red remains the same, light brown to medium brown (✳640), gold to off-white (✳712).

Another possible color combination is the following: change dark blue-green to black (✳310), light blue-green to light gray (✳415), red to dark gray (✳413), light brown to medium gray (✳414), gold to white blanc neige.

STITCH CHANGES: The areas other than the yellow background are too small for decorative stitches. To change the background stitch, use St. George and St. Andrew Cross stitch or Double Cross stitch.

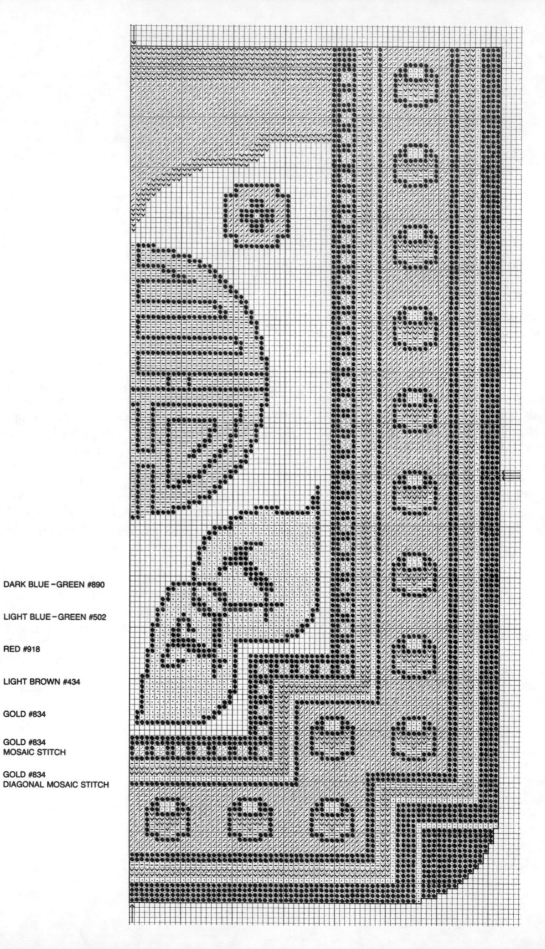

● DARK BLUE—GREEN #890

— LIGHT BLUE—GREEN #502

∨ RED #918

／ LIGHT BROWN #434

· GOLD #834

⦙ GOLD #834
MOSAIC STITCH

☐ GOLD #834
DIAGONAL MOSAIC STITCH

*Graph A*

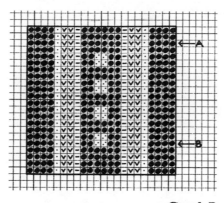

*Graph B*

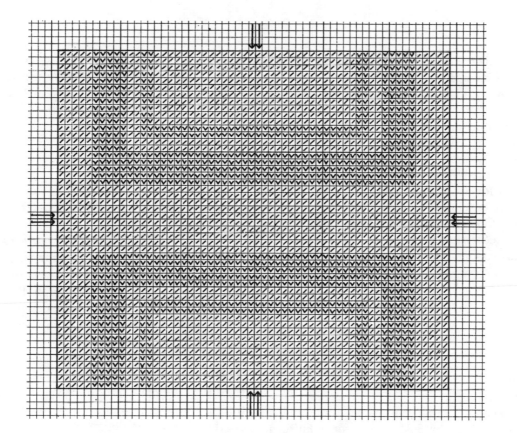

*Graph C*

# CHINESE GARDEN
# BELL PULL

## History

The design of the Chinese Garden bell pull is from a pair of Chinese silk-embroidered sleeves dating from the late Ch'ing (Manchu) dynasty of the nineteenth century. The emphasis on very wide sleeves, with one or more contrasting and elaborately embroidered borders on the sleeves, reveals a characteristic Chinese approach to the design and decoration of the *ch'ang-fu,* the elegant coat of the upper classes for wear when not at court. Although the *ch'ang-fu* developed from a Manchurian coat, the enduring Chinese influence as seen in the sleeve design and decoration suggests to what degree the Manchurian conquerors of China had been assimilated into Chinese culture by the nineteenth century.

## Canvas

The thread count for the design is 150 threads wide by 640 threads long.

If you choose 12 mesh canvas, cut and bind a piece of canvas 15½ by 56½ inches for a finished design approximately 12½ by 53½ inches.

If you choose 14 mesh canvas, cut and bind a piece of canvas 14 by 49 inches for a finished design approximately 11 by 46 inches.

If you choose 18 mesh canvas, cut and bind a piece of canvas 11½ by 38½ inches for a finished design approximately 8½ by 35½ inches.

## Stitching Directions

The graph is drawn in four parts—Graphs A, B, C, and D. See Figure 26.

Find and mark the center of your canvas with an indelible marker. Follow the arrows marked at the edges of the graph parts until the arrows intersect. These four squares, two on Graph B and two on Graph C, mark the center of the design.

Find and mark the center 4 meshes of your canvas with an indelible marker to correspond to the center four squares of the two graph parts. From these center points, count 75 threads to the left, 75 threads to the right, 320 threads to the top, and 320 threads to the bottom and mark these points, which are the edges of the design.

You are now ready to begin stitching. Counting from the center points, stitch Graph B and Graph C. Then stitch Graph A and Graph D in their appropriate places, as shown in Figure 26.

Stitch all parts of the design except the background. Fill in the background after you have completed the design from all four graph parts.

As an alternative method of laying out the bell pull, you can mark the edges of the design on the canvas, then stitch the four graph parts beginning with Graph A, then Graph B, then Graph C, then Graph D. If you prefer this method, check and recheck the thread count as you have marked it on the canvas.

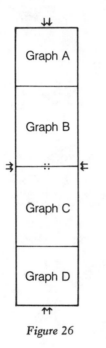

Figure 26

## Color and Stitch Key

The colors are brighter than those of the four embroideries from which the bell pull was adapted. They may approximate the original colors, which have since faded with age. Thread numbers refer to DMC pearl cotton. The location of the stitches used is noted on the key. See Plate 7.

## Finishing

To finish the bell pull refer to the instructions under Finishing (Bell Pull and Bell Pull Top Trim for the Chinese Garden bell pull).

## Creative Alternatives

DESIGN CHANGES: The bell pull can be divided into four pillows: first, the top building; second and third, each of the women; fourth, the bottom building. The pillows of the women form a pair and the pillows of the buildings make a second pair.

To make a pillow of the top building, add approximately 1 inch of background to the top edge of the bell pull. Fill in the space with blue water lines. Make the bottom edge of the pillow approximately 1 inch below the coral rock and green plant.

To make the woman with the coral costume into a pillow, use the top of the fence as the top edge of the pillow. Let the edge cut through the tree. Make the bottom edge of the pillow just below the blue rock on which the woman stands, but above the two ducks. Add approximately 1 to 1½ inches of background to the bottom edge of the pillow. Fill in the space with blue water lines.

To make the woman with the green costume into a pillow, use the area just above the fence and two ducks as the top edge of the pillow. Add approximately 2 inches of background to the top edge. Fill in the space with water lines and one or two small blue rocks. Make the bottom edge just below the blue leaf beneath the woman's costume. Omit the green leaves of the tree next to the blue leaf. Add approximately 1 inch of background to the bottom edge of the pillow. Fill in the space with blue water lines.

For a pillow of the bottom building, make the top edge of the pillow approximately 1 to 1½ inches above the top part of the building. Make the bottom edge approximately 1 inch below the bottom of the coral jar.

COLOR CHANGES: Try the following color combinations by changing the color key: change dark blue to dark brown (✳640 DMC pearl cotton), medium blue to medium brown (✳642), light blue to light brown (✳644), coral to rust (✳920), light coral to light rust (✳922). Black, medium gray, light gray, green, light green, brown, flesh, and white remain the same.

STITCH CHANGES: In place of Diagonal Mosaic stitch, try Milanese or Oriental stitch for the background.

103

| | LIGHT GREEN #368 | | BLACK #310 |
| | CORAL #350 | | MEDIUM GRAY #414 |
| | LIGHT CORAL #353 | | LIGHT GRAY #415 |
| | BROWN #640 | | DARK BLUE #798 |
| | FLESH #819 | | MEDIUM BLUE #799 |
| | WHITE BLANC NEIGE | | LIGHT BLUE #800 |
| | WHITE BLANC NEIGE DIAGONAL MOSAIC STITCH | | GREEN #987 (#3 PEARL COTTON) #367 (#5 PEARL COTTON) |

*Graph A*

Graph B

*Graph C*

*Graph D*

# CHINESE BUTTERFLIES BELL PULL

## History

The design for this bell pull comes from a nine-teenth-century pair of sleeves from a *ch'ang-fu* of the late Ch'ing (Manchu) dynasty, which ruled China from 1644 to 1912. Like the Chinese Garden bell pull, this design reflects those contrasting sleeve borders of the very wide sleeves of the *ch'ang-fu*. Although it is difficult to know when the Chinese chose decorative designs on their garments for pictorial beauty or for symbolism, the butterfly motif on these sleeves was a Chinese symbol for happiness. It was an appropriate designation for a garment worn by the upper classes when at leisure and not in court apparel.

## Canvas

The thread count for the design is 150 threads wide by 594 threads long.

If you choose 12 mesh canvas, cut and bind a piece of canvas 15½ by 52½ inches for a finished design approximately 12½ by 49½ inches.

If you choose 14 mesh canvas, cut and bind a piece of canvas 14 by 45½ inches for a finished design approximately 11 by 42½ inches.

If you choose 18 mesh canvas, cut and bind a piece of canvas 11½ by 36 inches for a finished design approximately 8½ by 33 inches.

## Stitching Directions

The graph is drawn in four parts—Graphs A, B, C, and D. See Figure 27.

Find and mark the center of your canvas with an indelible marker. Follow the arrows marked at the edges of the graph parts until the arrows intersect. These four squares, two on Graph B and two on Graph C, mark the center of the design.

Find and mark the center 4 meshes of your canvas with an indelible marker to correspond to the center four squares of the two graph parts. From these center points count 75 threads to the left, 75 threads to the right, 297 threads to the top, 297 threads to the bottom and mark these points, which are the edges of the design.

You are now ready to begin stitching. Counting from the center points, stitch Graph B and Graph

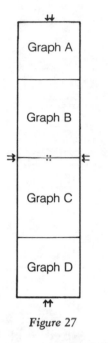

*Figure 27*

C. Then stitch Graph A and Graph D in their appropriate places as shown in Figure 27.

Stitch the dark gray outlines of the butterflies, flowers, and border from all four graph parts, then fill in the colors and decorative stitches. Finally, stitch the white background.

As an alternative method of laying out the bell pull, you can mark the edges of the design on the canvas, then stitch the four graph parts from top to bottom rather than from the center outward. If you prefer this method, check and recheck the thread count as you have marked it on the canvas.

## Color and Stitch Key

The colors here are more intense than those of the embroidery from which the bell pull was adapted, as the originals have faded with time. The thread numbers refer to DMC pearl cotton. The location of various decorative stitches is noted on the key. See Plate 17.

*Creative Alternatives*

DESIGN CHANGES: You can make a pillow using each butterfly. Stitch the butterfly and several flowers around the butterfly. Increase the size of the background to a generous square and add the border from the bell pull around the pillow. See Figure 28.

*Figure 28*

COLOR CHANGES: Make the bell pull predominantly brown by changing the color key as follows: change purple to light rust (⚡922 DMC pearl cotton), dark blue to dark brown (⚡640), medium blue to medium brown (⚡642), light blue to light brown (⚡644), gold to rust (⚡920). Dark gray, medium gray, light gray, and white remain the same.

STITCH CHANGES: Change Scotch stitch to Rhodes stitch. Change Alternating Mosaic stitch to two-tone light blue and white St. George and St. Andrew Cross stitch; change Diagonal Mosaic stitch to Milanese stitch or Oriental stitch.

*Graph A*

| | DARK GRAY #413 | | | DARK GRAY #413 CASHMERE STITCH | | Z | PURPLE #210 |
| | DARK GRAY #413 SLANTING GOBELIN STITCH OVER 2 MESHES | | X | MEDIUM GRAY #414 | | ∧ | PURPLE #210 SCOTCH STITCH OVER 4 MESHES |
| Ш | DARK GRAY #413 SCOTCH STITCH OVER 3 MESHES | | — | LIGHT GRAY #415 | | ● | DARK BLUE #798 |

| | DARK BLUE #798 SLANTING GOBELIN STITCH OVER 2 MESHES | | | LIGHT BLUE #800 ALTERNATING MOSAIC STITCH | | | WHITE BLANC NEIGE |
| | MEDIUM BLUE #799 | | | LIGHT BLUE #800 SLANTING GOBELIN STITCH OVER 2 MESHES | | | WHITE BLANC NEIGE DIAGONAL MOSAIC STITCH |
| | LIGHT BLUE #800 | | | GOLD #782 | | | |

*Graph B*

*Graph C*

*Graph D*

|  GOLD #733 | $\vee$ BLUE #501 | $|$ BLUE – GREEN #521 |
|---|---|---|
| $\cdot$ WHITE #260 | $/$ RED #930 | ☐ BLUE – GREEN #521 CROSS STITCH |

114

# CHINESE CLOISONNÉ PINCUSHION

## History

The design for this pincushion comes from a floral motif covering the cloisonné surface of an elephant-shaped box and cover from the Ch'ien Lung period (1735–96). Cloisonné is the technique of enameling where different-colored enamels are divided from one another by thin strips of metal previously soldered to the base. The chrysanthemum design which forms the background for this pincushion was a favored motif of Chinese cloisonné work symbolizing both autumn and a long life. By the eighteenth century, the copper divisions between the different-colored enamels were lavishly gilded at the same time that a wider variety of colors was introduced. The result was that the eighteenth-century Imperial Chinese workshops turned out vast quantities of cloisonné work superb in technique and brilliant in color, although not always as original as the earlier work.

## Canvas

The thread count for the design is 118 threads wide by 100 threads long.

To make a pincushion, cut and bind a piece of 18 mesh canvas 10 by 9 inches for a finished design approximately 7 by 6 inches.

To make a pillow, cut and bind a piece of 10 mesh canvas 15 by 13 inches for a finished design approximately 12 by 10 inches.

## Stitching Directions

Follow the arrows marked at the edges of the graph to find the four center squares on the graph. Find and mark the 4 center meshes of your canvas with an indelible marker to correspond to the graph. From these center points, count outward and lightly mark the edges of the design on your canvas.

You are now ready to begin stitching. Counting from the center outward, stitch the gold outlines, then fill in the various colors of the flower, and finally, stitch the background.

## Color and Stitch Key

The colors are approximately those of the original cloisonné. Yarn numbers refer to Paternayan yarn. The location of the stitches used is noted on the key. See Plate 2.

## Creative Alternatives

DESIGN AND STITCH CHANGES: On 10 mesh canvas the pincushion will make a pillow. Make the pincushion corners square and add the following border: 2-stitch border of gold, then 4-stitch border of blue, then 2-stitch border of gold, then 4-stitch border of white, then 2-stitch border of gold, then 12-stitch border of red. Stitch the gold borders in Slanting Gobelin stitch; stitch the blue border in Scotch stitch; stitch the white border in Fern stitch; stitch the red border in Double Cross stitch. Stitch the background in Diagonal Mosaic stitch.

COLOR CHANGES: Reverse the blue-green and white so that the leaves are blue-green and the background is white. Try the following combination for a black, brown, and white pincushion: change gold and blue to black (※220 Paternayan yarn), red to brown (※412), blue-green to light brown (※414). White remains the same.

# CHINESE ROSE
# MEDALLION PILLOW

## History

The design for this pillow comes from a floral detail of a Chinese nineteenth-century porcelain export ware known as Rose Medallion. Made and decorated in Canton, this famille rose pattern was called Rose Canton if the primary subject was floral design, or Rose Medallion if other subjects, primarily figures in mandarin clothes, filled the spaces inside the medallions. The detail used for the design of the pillow comes from the floral border around the medallion and might, at first glance, be confused with Rose Canton were it not for the strong emphasis on the medallion form of the design.

## Canvas

The thread count for the design is 228 threads square.

If you choose 14 mesh canvas, cut and bind a piece of canvas 19½ inches square for a finished design approximately 16½ inches square.

If you choose 18 mesh canvas, cut and bind a piece of canvas 15½ inches square for a finished design approximately 12½ inches square.

## Stitching Directions

The graph is drawn in quarters—Upper Left, Upper Right, Lower Left, or Lower Right according to its position in relation to the whole design.

Follow the two arrows marked at the edges of each graph quarter until they intersect. This intersection marks the square on each quarter where you should begin stitching. Together the four squares, one from each quarter, mark the center of the design.

Find and mark the center 4 meshes of your canvas with an indelible marker to correspond to the four center squares of the graph. From these center points, count outward and lightly mark the border of the design on the canvas.

You are now ready to begin stitching. Counting from the center points outward, stitch the rust border lines and dark gray outlines. Then fill in the flowers, leaves, birds, and borders. Finally, stitch the background. Stitch the entire design in Continental or Basketweave stitch.

## Color Key

The colors are close to those of the original bowl. Yarn numbers refer to Paternayan yarn. See Plate 15.

## Creative Alternatives

DESIGN CHANGES: The pillow would also be effective if you removed the center birds and flowers and added a monogram outlined in charcoal and worked in green, pink, blue, yellow, and rust.

A portion of the border can be used as a glasses case. See Figure 29. To make the shape fit the glasses case size of 3½ by 6½ inches, increase by several rows the light green area between the dark gray and rust lines. Use the rust line of 2 stitches and then increase by several rows the white border.

COLOR CHANGES: You might consider stitching the pillow in four values of blue ($\#$500, $\#$502, $\#$504, and $\#$506 Paternayan yarn) plus white. Use the darkest blue ($\#$500) for the outlines.

STITCH CHANGES: The pillow design is too detailed and the areas too small for effective use of decorative stitches. If you must incorporate one, use Diagonal Mosaic for the background.

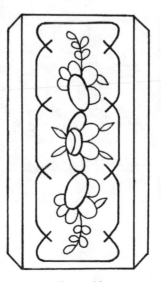

*Figure 29*

*Upper Left*

| | DARK GRAY #210 | | YELLOW #714 |
|---|---|---|---|
| | RUST #872 | | PINK #905 |

| Symbol | Color |
|--------|-------|
| ∨ | LIGHT PINK #964 |
| + | LIGHT BLUE #554 |
| · | LIGHT GREEN #665 |
| ⊙ | BLUE #553 |
| ╱ | GREEN #664 |
| ☐ | WHITE #260 |

*Upper Right*

*Lower Left*

*Lower Right*

*Chinese Purse*

# CHINESE PURSE

## History

The design for this purse consists of details from a Chinese rug of the eighteenth century with the Chinese character shou (long life) portrayed in its usual mirror-image form in a medallion. The floral border surrounding the medallion dates back to the Ming dynasty (1368–1644) but was still popular in the Ch'ien Lung period (1735–96) as a stylized representation of sprays of pomegranate, the classical Chinese symbol for fertility. On the original rug, this floral border was slightly embossed to emphasize its effect, which on a larger surface would otherwise have faded into the background.

## Canvas

The thread count for the purse body is 162 threads wide by 150 threads long. The purse top is a separate piece for which the thread count is 58 threads wide by 50 threads long.

If you choose 14 mesh canvas, cut and bind two pieces of canvas 14½ by 14 inches for finished designs approximately 11½ by 11 inches. Also cut and bind two pieces of canvas for the top, 7 by 6½ inches for finished designs 4 by 3½ inches.

If you choose 18 mesh canvas, cut and bind two pieces of canvas 12 by 11½ inches for finished designs approximately 9 by 8½ inches. Also cut and bind two pieces of canvas for the top, 6 by 5½ inches for finished designs approximately 3 by 2½ inches.

## Stitching Directions

The graph for the purse is drawn in two parts—Graph A and Graph B. Graph A represents the right half of the purse body. Graph B is the purse top. You will work first with Graph A and the two pieces of canvas for the purse body. Put aside the two pieces of canvas for the purse top.

THE PURSE BODY: Follow the arrows marked at the edges of Graph A until they intersect. These two intersection squares correspond to the center of the canvas and mark the points where you will begin stitching.

Mark the center of your first piece of canvas with an indelible marker to correspond to the two graph intersection squares. Counting from these canvas meshes, mark the right, top, and bottom edges of the design on your canvas. The number of threads from the center to the right edge of the design should be 81, half the horizontal thread count. The number of threads from the top edge of the design to the bottom edge should be 150, the vertical thread count.

Mark the center meshes and the right, top, and bottom edges of the design on your second piece of canvas so that it is identical to the first.

You are now ready to begin stitching. Stitch the first piece of canvas. Counting from the center points, stitch all design parts of Graph A except the Diagonal Mosaic stitch background. Stitch the design for the left half in a mirror image of the right half. Now fill in the background.

Stitch the second piece of canvas exactly as you stitched the first half. You have now completed the two pieces of the purse body.

THE PURSE TOP: Follow the arrows marked at the edges of Graph B to find the four center squares. Mark, with an indelible marker, the 4 center meshes of one piece of canvas to correspond to the four center squares on the graph. From the center points, count outward and lightly mark the left, right, top, and bottom edges of the design on the canvas.

Mark the center meshes and design edges on your second piece of canvas so that it is identical to the first.

You are now ready to begin stitching. Counting from the center points, stitch Graph B. Repeat Graph B on your second piece of canvas. You have now completed the two purse tops.

*Figure 30*

## Color and Stitch Key

The colors I chose are from the various original rugs of which the purse is an adaptation. Thread numbers refer to DMC pearl cotton. The stitches used are noted on the key. See Plate 8.

## Finishing

To finish the purse, refer to the instructions under Finishing (Purse with Needlepoint Top).

## Creative Alternatives

DESIGN CHANGES: The purse design will make a pillow if all corners are either square or rounded.

A panel of center medallions, one beneath another, would make a bell pull. Divide the medallions with stripes, as in Figure 30.

COLOR CHANGES: Black and white would be good substitute colors for the purse, either a white design on a black background or a black design on a white background.

You can make a black, brown, and white purse by using the colors as follows: change the present

● WHITE ECRU    □ LIGHT BROWN #642 DIAGONAL MOSAIC STITCH    ⁄ LIGHT BROWN #642

*Graph A*

white areas to black (✳310 DMC pearl cotton); change the present brown Continental or Basket-weave areas to ecru; change the brown Diagonal Mosaic background to rust brown (✳433).

Any two or three colors can be used in one of the above ways.

STITCH CHANGES: Any background stitch used here must be small-scale, such as Mosaic stitch, Cross stitch, or St. George and St. Andrew Cross stitch. The areas are too small and the design too busy for any larger-scale stitches.

If you stitch the bell pull alternative mentioned above, you could incorporate Ray stitch or Rhodes stitch as part of the stripes between medallions.

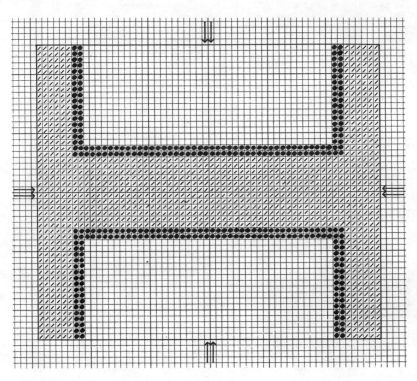

*Graph B*

126

# MONGOL PURSE

## History

The design for this purse comes from a Mongol rug of the late eighteenth century. Although Mongol rugs of this period may appear to have a somewhat Chinese character, they have an independent history of development of design and color going back to medieval times. The bold Mongol designs and colors are more simple and robust than Chinese ones and reflect the Mongols' nomadic life. Lacking the indigo plant of China, the Mongols had no ready access to the source of blue so common as the ground for Chinese rugs. Instead basic Mongol colors are often those found in this design (red, dark brown, and white), sometimes with the addition of very bright colors. The geometric medallion in the center of this design with its triangular sections and scalloped inner sides at each corner reflects the straightforward and vigorous approach to design of the Mongols.

## Canvas

The thread count for the purse body is 156 threads wide by 134 threads long. The purse top is a separate piece for which the thread count is 58 threads wide by 50 threads long.

If you choose 14 mesh canvas, cut and bind two pieces of canvas 14 by 12½ inches for finished designs approximately 11 by 9½ inches. Also cut and bind two pieces of canvas for the top, 7 by 6½ inches for finished designs 4 by 3½ inches.

If you choose 18 mesh canvas, cut and bind two pieces of canvas 11½ by 10½ inches for finished designs approximately 8½ by 7½ inches. Also cut and bind two pieces of canvas for the top, 6 by 5½ inches for finished designs approximately 3 by 2½ inches.

## Stitching Directions

The graph for the purse is drawn in two parts—Graph A and Graph B. Graph A represents the right half of the purse body. Graph B is the purse top. You will work first with Graph A and the two pieces of canvas for the purse body. Put aside the two pieces of canvas for the purse top.

THE PURSE BODY: Follow the arrows marked at the edges of Graph A until they intersect. These two intersection squares correspond to the center of the canvas and are the points where you will begin stitching.

*Graph A*

*Persian Elephants Pillow*

Plate 11

*Plate 12*          *Japanese Resting Pheasant Pillow*
                    *Japanese Flying Pheasant Pillow*

*Japanese Mandarin Duck Pillow*                    *Plate 13*

*Plate 14*          *Persian Falconer Pillow*
                    *Persian Hunter Pillow*

*Persian Rug*

Plate 15

Plate 16          *Japanese Woodblock Print Pillow*

*Korean Tortoise and Snake Pillow*

Plate 17

*Plate 18*     *Indian Yantra Pillow*                    *Indian Astronomical Chart Pillow*
                                                              *Indian Egg Pillow*

Mark the center of your first piece of canvas with an indelible marker to correspond to the two graph intersection squares. Counting from these canvas meshes, mark the right, top, and bottom edges of the design on your canvas. The number of threads from the center to the right edge of the design should be 78, half the horizontal thread count. The number of threads from the top edge of the design to the bottom edge should be 134 threads, the vertical thread count.

Mark the center meshes and the right, top, and bottom edges of the design on your second piece of canvas so that it is identical to the first.

You are now ready to begin stitching. Stitch the first piece of canvas. Counting from the center points, stitch all design parts of Graph A except the Diagonal Mosaic stitch background. Stitch the design for the left half in a mirror image of the right half. Now fill in the background.

Stitch the second piece of canvas exactly as you stitched the first half. You have now completed the two pieces of the purse body.

THE PURSE TOP: Follow the arrows marked at the edges of Graph B to find the four center squares. Mark, with an indelible marker, the 4 center meshes of one piece of canvas to correspond to the four center squares on the graph. From the center points, count outward and lightly mark the left, right, top, and bottom edges of the design on the canvas.

Mark the center meshes and design edges on your second piece of canvas so that it is identical to the first.

You are now ready to begin stitching. Counting from the center points, stitch Graph B. Repeat Graph B on your second piece of canvas. You have now completed the two purse tops.

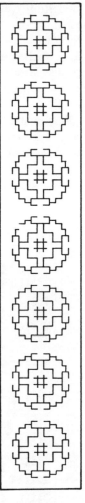

*Figure 31*

## Finishing

To finish the purse refer to the instructions under Finishing (Purse with Needlepoint Top).

## Color and Stitch Key

The three colors I chose are from the two original rugs of which the purse is an adaptation. Thread numbers refer to DMC pearl cotton. The stitches used are noted on the key. See Plate 8.

## Creative Alternatives

DESIGN CHANGES: Use the design for a pillow by squaring all of the corners like the upper part of the purse or rounding all four edges like the lower part of the purse.

● DARK BROWN #938    ◿ WHITE ECRU    · RED #918    ☐ RED #918 DIAGONAL MOSAIC STITCH

129

A single center medallion would make a pincushion on 18 mesh canvas.

A panel of center medallions, one beneath another, would make a bell pull. After you have stitched the medallions, stitch a simple border of several stripes of brown and red around the medallions. See Figure 31.

COLOR CHANGES: If you use black or dark brown and ecru or white, any third color will work. A good combination for this design would be black (⋇310 DMC pearl cotton), ecru, and brown (⋇433), as in the Persian glasses case. Another good combination would be dark brown (⋇938), ecru, and blue (⋇322).

STITCH CHANGES: Any small-scale stitch will work well as a background stitch. St. George and St. Andrew Cross stitch would be one such choice. Avoid a large-scale decorative stitch, as it would overpower the design.

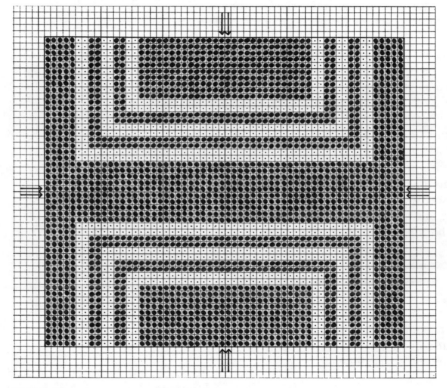

*Graph B*

# KOREAN TORTOISE AND SNAKE PILLOW

## History

The unusual design for this pillow comes from a wall painting in the tomb of the Four Cardinal Deities in T'ung-kou. At the time this painting was made, between the sixth and seventh centuries, this area of northern Korea known as Koguryo (37 B.C.–668 A.D.) was the largest of the three kingdoms which made up ancient Korea. Koguryo art reflected the influence of China at the same time that it began to develop a distinctive indigenous style. That Korean style can be seen here in the unusual vigor of this design depicting an intertwined tortoise and snake. The confronting heads of the tortoise and snake form a heraldic design set within the medallion formed by the writhing body of the snake. The result is quite different from anything in Chinese painting of the same period.

## Canvas

The thread count for the design is 250 threads wide by 210 threads long.

If you choose 14 mesh canvas, cut and bind a piece of canvas 21 by 18 inches for a finished design approximately 18 by 15 inches.

If you choose 18 mesh canvas, cut and bind a piece of canvas 17 by 14½ inches for a finished design approximately 14 by 11½ inches.

## Stitching Directions

The graph is drawn in quarters—Upper Left, Upper Right, Lower Left, or Lower Right according to its position in relation to the whole design.

Follow the two arrows marked at the edges of each graph quarter until they intersect. This intersection marks the square on each quarter where you should begin stitching. Together, the four squares, one from each quarter, mark the center of the design.

Find and mark the center 4 meshes of your canvas with an indelible marker to correspond to the four center squares of the graph. From these center points, count outward and lightly mark the edges of the design on the canvas.

You are now ready to begin stitching. Counting from the center outward, first stitch the dark gray outlines, then fill in the various colors, and finally, stitch the background.

## Color and Stitch Key

The colors are similar to those used in the original painting. Yarn numbers refer to Paternayan yarn. The location of various stitches is noted on the key. The key instructs you to stitch the Tile stitch background in light green, white, and gray. Referring to the stitch diagrams for Tile stitch, work steps 1 and 2 in light green, step 3 in white, and step 4 in light gray. See Plate 17.

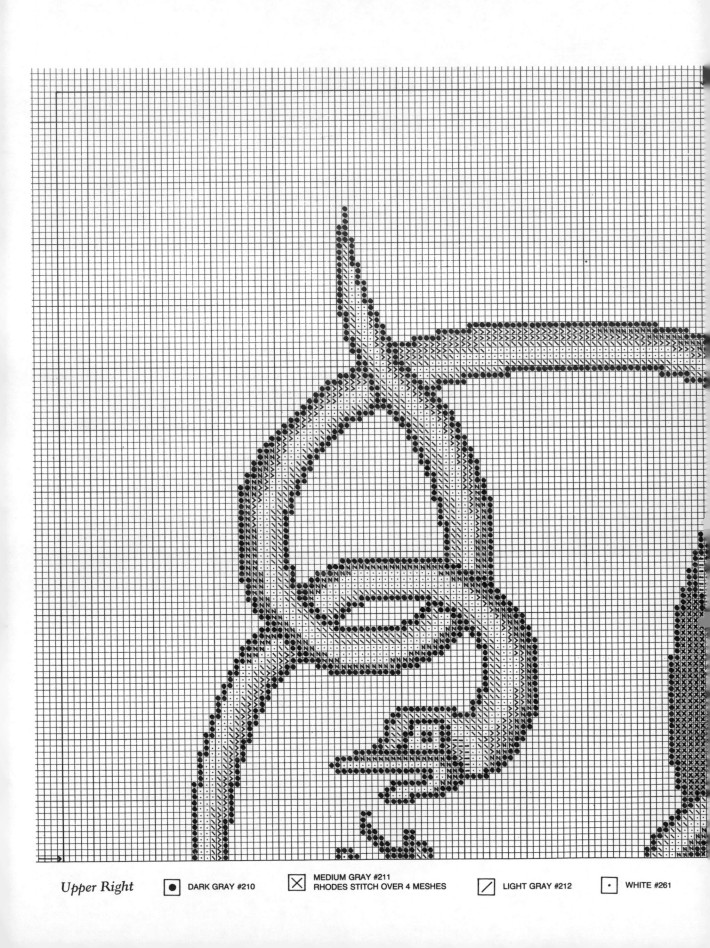

*Upper Right*    ● DARK GRAY #210    ⊠ MEDIUM GRAY #211 RHODES STITCH OVER 4 MESHES    ╱ LIGHT GRAY #212    · WHITE #261

*Lower Right*

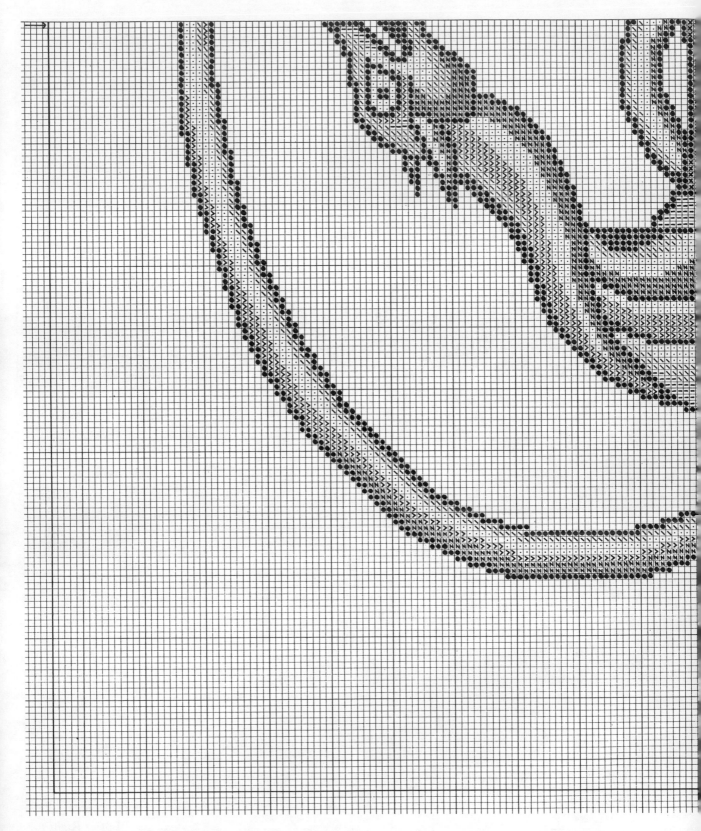

*Upper Left*

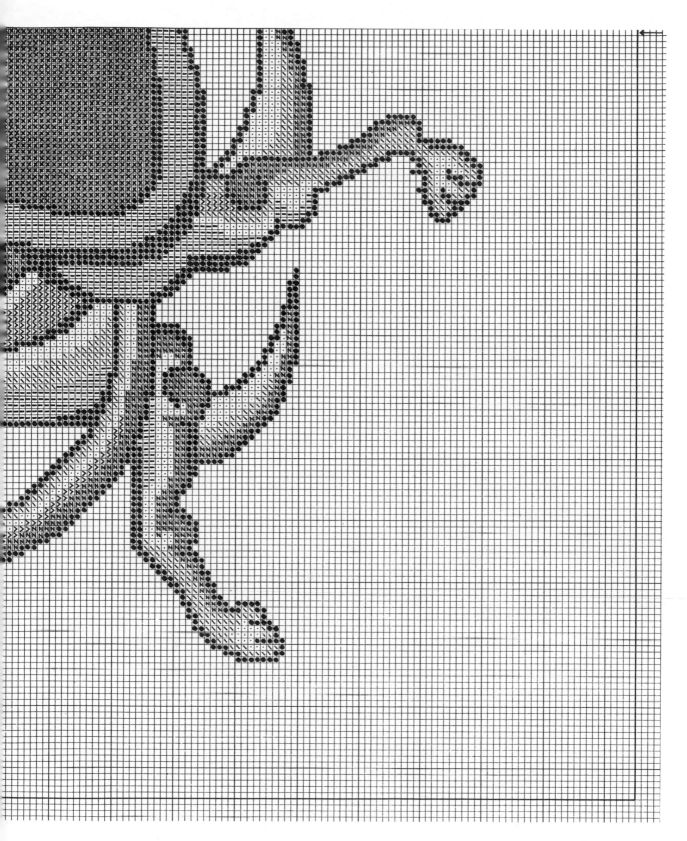

*Lower Left*

## Creative Alternatives

DESIGN CHANGES: Add a 4-inch border around the design. Vary the border first with a stripe of charcoal gray and then with stripes of the other colors.

COLOR CHANGES: Change the colors as follows: charcoal gray to dark blue (✳500 Paternayan yarn), medium gray to medium blue (✳502), light gray and green to light blue (✳505), rust and light orange to dark red (✳930). White and light green remain the same.

STITCH CHANGES: Change the tortoise's shell to Double Cross stitch; change the background to Scotch stitch using three colors.

If you use the color changes, stitch the background in two-tone Oriental stitch or Jacquard stitch.

# KOREAN CRANES PILLOW

## History

The design for this pillow comes from a Korean vase of about 1150 A.D. from Maebyong. This was during the Koryo period (918–1392), distinguished in the arts by its fine ceramics collected by Sung connoisseurs in China. This design of roundels with cranes covers the entire surface of the Korean inlaid celadon vase from which it is taken. The crane was considered the companion of the Taoist Immortals. It was a symbol of immortality and also functioned as a messenger of the god of longevity. Buddhism had first entered Korea from China in 372 A.D. By the Koryo period, it was the dominant religion, and its monasteries were the major centers of inspiration for learning and for art as in the design shown here.

## Canvas

The thread count for the design is 216 threads square.

If you choose 14 mesh canvas, cut and bind a piece of canvas 18½ inches square for a finished design approximately 15½ inches square.

If you choose 18 mesh canvas, cut and bind a piece of canvas 15 inches square for a finished design 12 inches square.

## Stitching Directions

The graph is drawn in quarters—Upper Left, Upper Right, Lower Left, or Lower Right according to its position in relation to the whole design.

Follow the two arrows marked at the edges of each graph quarter until they intersect. This intersection marks the square on each quarter where you should begin stitching. Together the four squares, one from each quarter, mark the center of the design.

Find and mark the center 4 meshes of your canvas with an indelible marker to correspond to the four center squares of the graph. From these center points, count outward and lightly mark the edges of the design on the canvas.

You are now ready to begin stitching. Stitch from the center points outward, counting and working the outlines and shapes of the design and then filling in the background.

## Color and Stitch Key

The original colors are celadon, white, and brown. Yarn numbers refer to Paternayan yarn. The location of the stitches used is noted on the key. See Plate 2.

## Creative Alternatives

DESIGN CHANGES:  Use one motif as a pincushion.
Make either a round pincushion using the circle
around the cranes as the edge, or a square pincushion placing the circle inside a square as in Figure
32. These same designs would also make small pillows if stitched on 10 mesh canvas.

*Figure 32*

A panel of cranes, one beneath the other, could
also make a bell pull. See Figure 33.

COLOR CHANGES:  Leave the brown the same and
reverse the blue-green and white so that the cranes
and details are blue-green and the background is
white.

Using brown and white, most soft colors will
work well as a third color. Try brown, white, and
dusty pink (✻923 Paternayan yarn) or brown,
white, and gold (✻743).

STITCH CHANGES:  Try Woven stitch, Woven
stitch variation, or a two-tone St. George and St.
Andrew Cross stitch as a background.

*Figure 33*

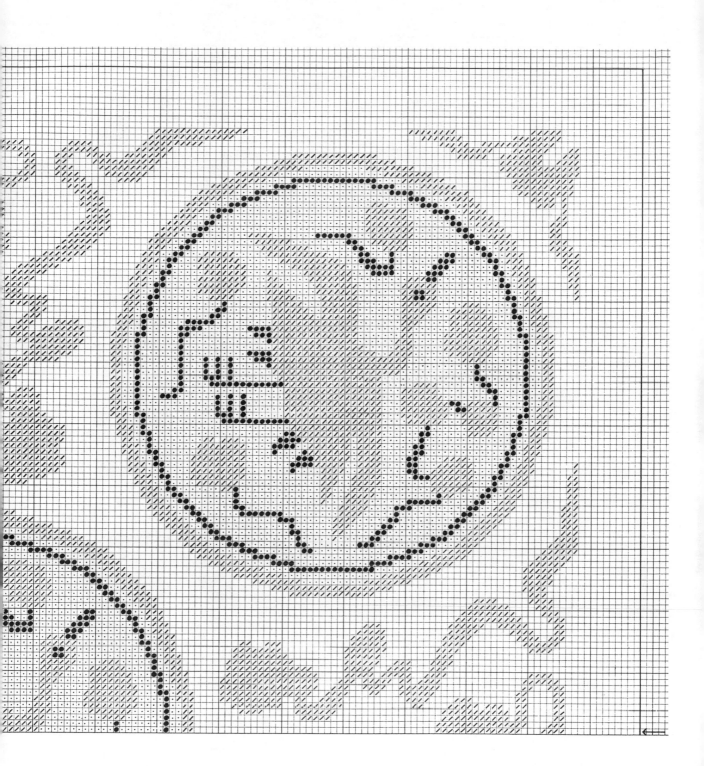

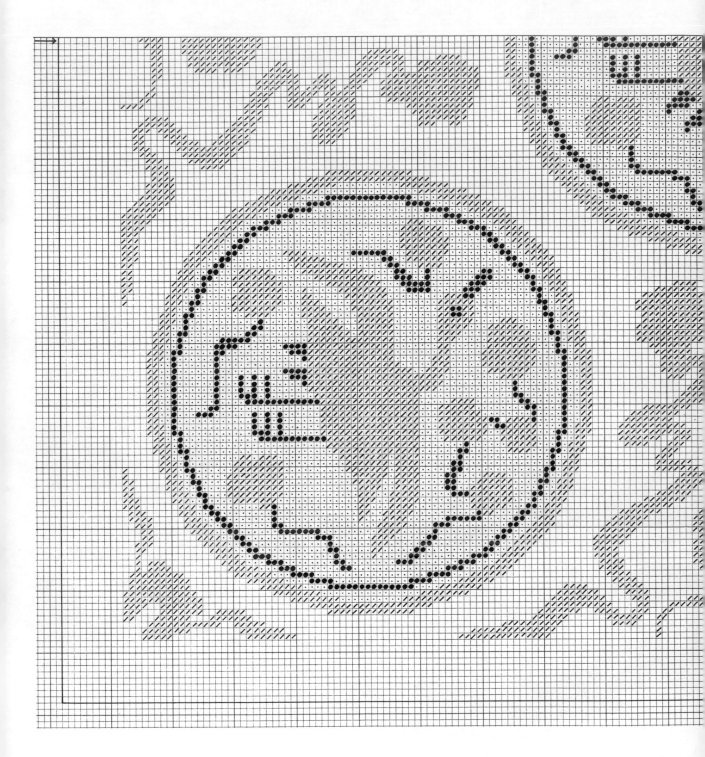

*Lower Left*

⬤ BROWN #452     ╱ WHITE #260

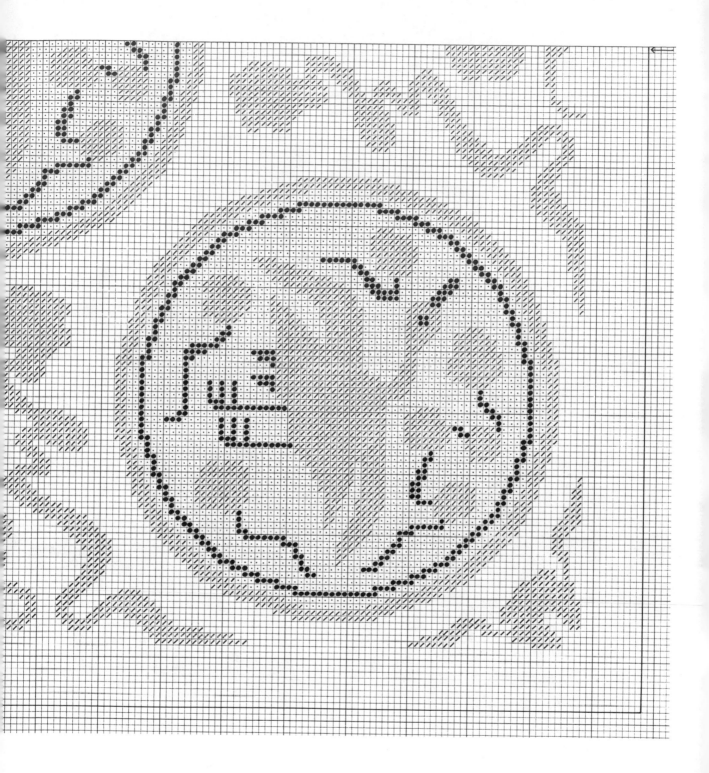

*Lower Right*

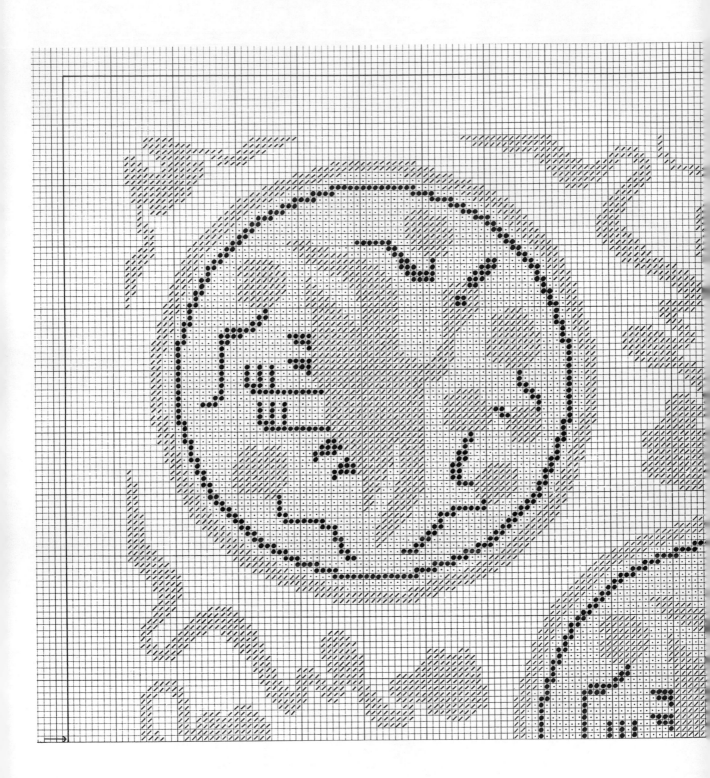

Upper Left

# KOREAN PINCUSHION

## History

The design for this pincushion comes from a Korean inlaid celadon ceramic pillow dating from the middle of the twelfth century during the Koryo period. The pincushion reproduces the abstract lotus blossom (recognizable by its individual seed pods in the center of the flower) which forms the design within one of the four medallions covering each side of the pillow. The lotus is the symbol of summer as well as of creativity and purity because Buddhas sit upon thrones of lotus flowers. The oblong, square-cornered ceramic pillow was used throughout East Asia and Japan, although it appears to a Westerner as the opposite of comfortable.

## Canvas

The thread count for the design is 110 threads wide by 146 threads long.

To make a pincushion, cut and bind a piece of 18 mesh canvas 9 by 11 inches for a finished design approximately 6 by 8 inches.

To make a pillow, cut and bind a piece of 10 mesh canvas 14 by 17½ inches for a finished design approximately 11 by 14½ inches.

## Stitching Directions

Follow the arrows marked at the edges of the graph to find the four center squares on the graph. Find and mark the 4 center meshes of your canvas with an indelible marker to correspond to the graph. From these center points, count outward and lightly mark the edges of the design on your canvas.

You are now ready to begin stitching. Counting from the center outward, stitch the brown and white design and then fill in the blue-green background. Stitch the entire design in Continental or Basketweave stitch.

## Color Key

The colors of the original design are celadon, white, and brown. Yarn numbers refer to Paternayan yarn. See Plate 2.

## Creative Alternatives

DESIGN AND STITCH CHANGES: The design will make a pillow on 10 or 12 mesh canvas. For a different pillow, use the center of the design, omitting the border. Make the design square by adding

*Figure 34*

2-stitch brown Slanting Gobelin border, then a 2-inch Tile stitch border. See Figure 35. Stitch steps 1 and 2 in white, step 3 in blue-green, step 4 in brown. Stitch the background in Diagonal Mosaic stitch.

COLOR CHANGES: See Korean Cranes Pillow color changes.

sufficient background. Add a 2-stitch brown Slanting Gobelin border, then a 2-inch border of Scotch stitch using three colors. See Figure 34. Stitch step 1 in blue-green, step 2 in white, step 3 in brown. Stitch the background in Diagonal Mosaic stitch.

For another version, stitch the whole design, then expand the background to a rectangle. Add a

*Figure 35*

● BROWN #452    ╱ WHITE #260    ☐ BLUE – GREEN #523

# JAPANESE IMARI PILLOW

## History

This design is taken from a Japanese Imari porcelain bowl of the late Edo (Tokugawa) period (1615–1868). The term Imari comes from the ceramic center and seaport from which this porcelain was shipped to Europe and China beginning in the seventeenth century. Imari porcelain, made in the Arita area, is easily distinguished by its elaborately designed and deeply colored glazes. Imari designs drew their inspiration from the brightly colored textiles with abstract floral and geometric designs favored by the urban classes of the Edo period. Imari designs consequently transfer very well back to fabrics, such as needlepoint, as is illustrated by the example here.

## Canvas

The thread count for the pillow is 228 threads in diameter.

If you choose 14 mesh canvas, cut and bind a piece of canvas 19½ inches square for a finished design approximately 16½ inches in diameter.

If you choose 18 mesh canvas, cut and bind a piece of canvas 15½ inches square for a finished design approximately 12½ inches in diameter.

## Stitching Directions

Find and mark the center of your canvas with an indelible marker. Follow the two arrows marked at the edges of the graph until they intersect. This square corresponds to the center of your canvas and marks the place you will begin stitching. Count from this square to the right-hand border of the design and mark this border lightly. The number of threads marked on your canvas from the center point to the right-hand border should equal 114, half the thread count. Returning to the center point, repeat the process from the center to the lower border. Again the number of threads marked on your canvas should be 114.

You are now ready to begin stitching. The Imari pillow is a four-way design. The graph represents the lower right quarter of the finished design. Stitch this quarter and then repeat it in a mirror image.

You will now have completed half of the design. Stitch the second half of the design in a mirror image to the first half.

Stitch the entire design in Continental or Basketweave stitch.

## Color Key

The colors used are similar to those found in Imari plates and jars. Yarn numbers refer to Paternayan yarn. See Plate 4.

## Creative Alternatives

DESIGN CHANGES: Stitch the center medallion. Marking the end of each crisscross section away from the center is a short red strip. Connect the four red strips by stitching 3 rows of red so that the strips form a border surrounding the medallion. This eliminates the four motifs radiating straight out from the center medallion. Stitch the crisscross section of the design so that it forms a background completely surrounding the medallion. Add a narrow white border and then a wider dark blue border. See Figure 36.

*Figure 36*

COLOR CHANGES: Stitch the design in five values of blue (✳510, ✳511, ✳512, ✳513, and ✳514 Paternayan yarn) plus white, or in five values of rust (✳870, ✳871, ✳872, ✳873, and ✳874) plus white.

STITCH CHANGES: The pillow design is too detailed and the areas too small for effective use of decorative stitches.

| ● | BLUE #500 | V | RED #930 | / | GOLD #752 | | WHITE #263 |
|---|---|---|---|---|---|---|---|
| · | LIGHT BLUE #505 | I | LIGHT RED #932 | Z | GREEN #603 | | |

# JAPANESE RESTING PHEASANT PILLOW

## History

The design for this pillow as well as for the Japanese Flying Pheasant pillow is freely adapted from a series of sliding door panels (fusumas) painted in the sixteenth century by Kano Motonobu. In the previous century, the theme of birds and flowers had been introduced into Japanese painting. The Kano school began a tradition of painting which brought this theme to its fullest development by careful use of space, color, and design, as can be seen here. Both pheasants, although in different ways, relate well to the rocks (with spots of lichen) beneath them, and to the branches from the rosebushes which surround them. The bright red plumage of the pheasants contrasts brilliantly with the other subdued colors here, as it does in the original painting.

## Canvas

The thread count for the design is 352 threads wide by 280 threads long.

If you choose 14 mesh canvas, cut and bind a piece of canvas 28½ by 23 inches for a finished design approximately 25½ by 20 inches.

If you choose 18 mesh canvas, cut and bind a piece of canvas 22½ by 18½ inches for a finished design approximately 19½ by 15½ inches.

## Stitching Directions

The graph is drawn in quarters—Upper Left, Upper Right, Lower Left, or Lower Right according to its position in relation to the whole design.

Follow the two arrows marked at the edges of each graph quarter until they intersect. This intersection marks the square on each quarter where you should begin stitching. Together the four squares, one from each quarter, mark the center of the design.

Find and mark the center 4 meshes of your canvas with an indelible marker to correspond to the four center squares of the graph. From these center points, count outward and lightly mark the edges of the design on the canvas.

CHARCOAL GRAY #221

MEDIUM BLUE-GREEN #522

MEDIUM BLUE-GREEN #522, LIGHT BLUE-GREEN #5
CROSSED CORNERS STITCH

DARK BLUE-GREEN #521

LIGHT BLUE-GREEN #523

RED #843

| | LIGHT BROWN #442 | C | RUST #883 | O | GOLD #752 | + | GREEN #603 | · | WHITE #261 | *Lower Right* |
| • | BROWN #411 | S | GRAY #202 | I | LIGHT GOLD #754 | \ | LIGHT GREEN #604 | | WHITE #261 ORIENTAL STITCH | |

*Upper Left*

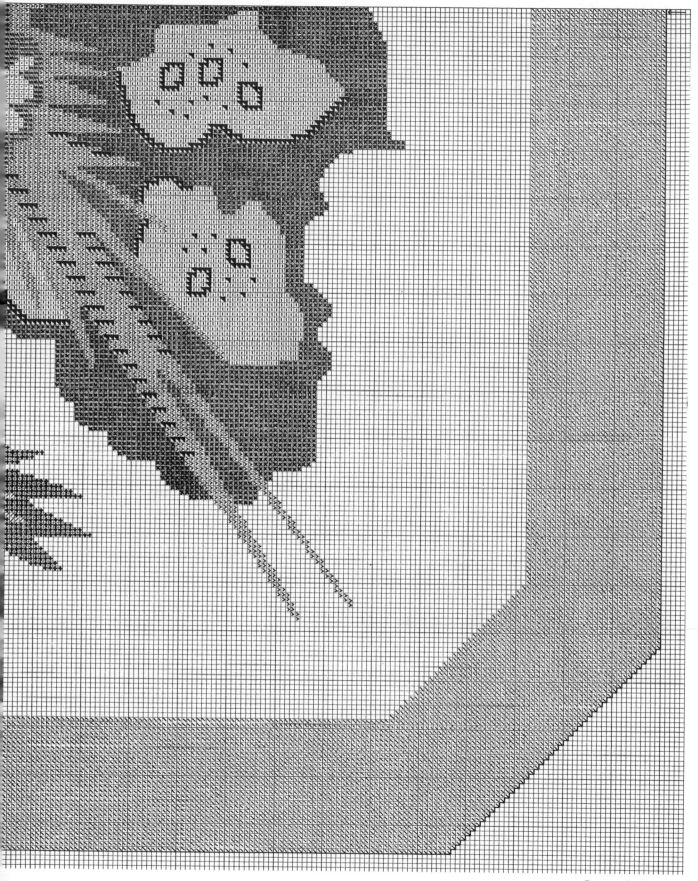

Now you are ready to begin stitching. Stitch from the center points outward, counting and working first the bird and the rock on which he stands, then the flowers, branches, and other decorations surrounding him. If you want to include your initials, refer to the alphabet in the Appendix and add the appropriate owner's-mark initials in the approximate positions in which they appear on the finished sample. Next stitch the border and finally the background.

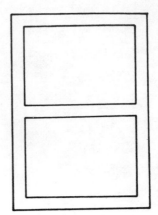

*Figure 37*

## Color and Stitch Key

The colors are similar to those in the original screen. Yarn numbers refer to Paternayan yarn. The location of decorative stitches is listed in the key. The key instructs you to stitch the Crossed Corners border in medium blue-green and light blue-green. Referring to the stitch diagrams for Crossed Corners stitch, work step 1 of the stitch in medium blue-green and step 2 in light blue-green. See Plate 12.

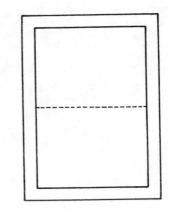

*Figure 38*

## Creative Alternatives

DESIGN CHANGES: For a smaller pillow, omit the border. Make the corners square if you want that shape.

You can combine the Resting Pheasant pillow and the Flying Pheasant pillow to make a rug. Use the following procedure: Treat the eight parts of the two graphs as one design with the resting pheasant on top of the flying pheasant. Leave the borders in place, but make the edges of each design square. See Figure 37. Or you may omit the borders and make the corners of the design square so that you can join the two pillows into one design. When you have stitched the two designs together, add a blue-green border to the rug. See Figure 38. Stitch the rug on 10 mesh canvas.

COLOR CHANGES: Change all light, medium, and dark blue-green areas to light, medium, and dark brown (✚443, ✚442, and ✚441 Paternayan yarn); also change the pheasant's red wings and breast to rust (✚480).

STITCH CHANGES: Any diagonal stitch such as Milanese or Jacquard would work well in place of Oriental stitch for the background. Any cross stitch over 4 meshes or Scotch stitch would work well for the border. If you combine the two pillows to make a rug, stitch the whole rug in Continental or Basket-weave stitch.

154

# JAPANESE FLYING PHEASANT PILLOW

## History

See the history under the Japanese Resting Pheasant pillow.

## Canvas

The thread count for the design is 352 threads wide by 280 threads long.

If you choose 14 mesh canvas, cut and bind a piece of canvas 28½ by 23 inches for a finished design approximately 25½ by 20 inches.

If you choose 18 mesh canvas, cut and bind a piece of canvas 22½ by 18½ inches for a finished design approximately 19½ by 15½ inches.

## Stitching Directions

The graph is drawn in quarters—Upper Left, Upper Right, Lower Left, or Lower Right according to its position in relation to the whole design.

Follow the two arrows marked at the edges of each graph quarter until they intersect. This intersection marks the square on each quarter where you should begin stitching. Together the four squares, one from each quarter, mark the center of the design.

Find and mark the center 4 meshes of your canvas with an indelible marker to correspond to the four center squares of the graph. From these center points, count outward and lightly mark the edges of the design on the canvas.

Now you are ready to begin stitching. Stitch from the center points outward, counting and working first the bird and the rock on which he stands, then the flowers, branches, and other decorations surrounding him. If you want to include your initials, refer to the alphabet in the Appendix and add the appropriate owner's-mark initials in the approximate positions in which they appear on the finished sample. Next stitch the border and finally the background.

## Color and Stitch Key

The colors are similar to those in the original screen. Yarn numbers refer to Paternayan yarn. The location of decorative stitches is listed on the key. The key instructs you to stitch the Crossed Corners border in medium blue-green and light blue-green. Referring to the stitch diagrams for Crossed Corners stitch, work step 1 of the stitch in medium blue-green and step 2 in light blue-green. See Plate 12.

## Creative Alternatives

See the Japanese Resting Pheasant pillow under Creative Alternatives.

*Upper Right*

*Lower Right*

| | | | | | | | | |
|---|---|---|---|---|---|---|---|---|
| ● | BROWN #411 | C | RUST #883 | O | GOLD #752 | + | GREEN #603 | · WHITE #261 |
| H | LIGHT BROWN #442 | S | GRAY #202 | I | LIGHT GOLD #754 | \ | LIGHT GREEN #604 | WHITE #261 ORIENTAL STITCH |

*Upper Left*

# JAPANESE MANDARIN DUCK PILLOW

## History

This design is taken from a detail of a painting, *Mandarin Ducks and Snow-Covered Reeds*, painted by Ito Jakuchu (1716–1800) toward the middle of his life. In the colors and posture of the duck, the cold of winter is very evident. Nonetheless, the mandarin duck, as the symbol of married happiness, adds a glow of internal warmth to this otherwise chilly scene. The placement of the angular reeds suggests why Ito Jakuchu was famous for his sense of design.

## Canvas

The thread count for the design is 196 threads in diameter.

If you choose 14 mesh canvas, cut and bind a piece of canvas 17 inches square for a finished design 14 inches in diameter.

If you choose 18 mesh canvas, cut and bind a piece of canvas 14 inches square for a finished design approximately 11 inches in diameter.

## Stitching Directions

The graph is drawn in quarters—Upper Left, Upper Right, Lower Left, or Lower Right according to its position in relation to the whole design.

Follow the two arrows marked at the edges of each graph quarter until they intersect. This intersection marks the square on each quarter where you should begin stitching. Together, the four squares, one from each quarter, mark the center of the design.

Find and mark the center 4 meshes of your canvas with an indelible marker to correspond to the four center squares of the graph. From these center points, count outward and lightly mark the edges of the design on the canvas.

You are now ready to begin stitching. Counting from the center outward, stitch first the duck and then the water lines and branches. If you wish to in-

clude your initials, refer to the alphabet in the Appendix and add the appropriate owner's-mark initials in the approximate positions in which they appear on the finished sample. Finally, stitch the background.

## Color and Stitch Key

The colors are approximately those used in the original painting. Thread numbers refer to DMC pearl cotton. The location of stitches used is listed on the key. See Plate 13.

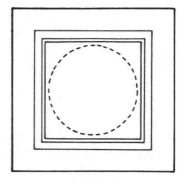

*Figure 39*

## Creative Alternatives

DESIGN AND STITCH CHANGES: Stitch the pillow as a square and add a border in the following pattern: 2-stitch dark brown border of Slanting Gobelin stitch, 4-stitch orange border of Crossed Corners stitch, 16-stitch rust border of Double Cross stitch. Change the background stitch from St. George and St. Andrew Cross stitch to Oriental, Milanese, or Diagonal Mosaic stitch. See Figure 39.

COLOR CHANGES: For another color combination try the following: black, dark brown, medium brown, light brown, and white remain the same; change rust to purple (✳208 DMC pearl cotton), orange to blue (✳798), light orange to light blue (✳800).

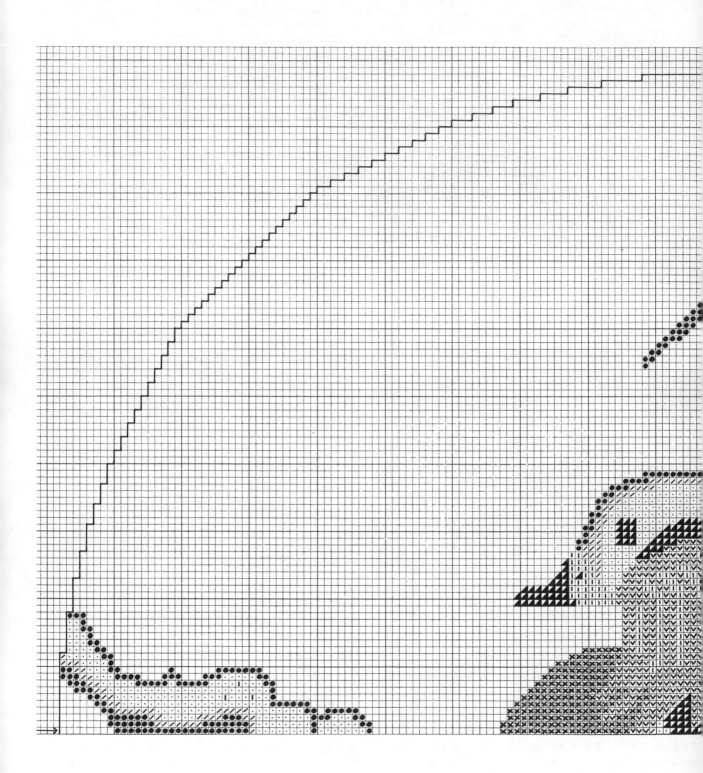

*Upper Left*

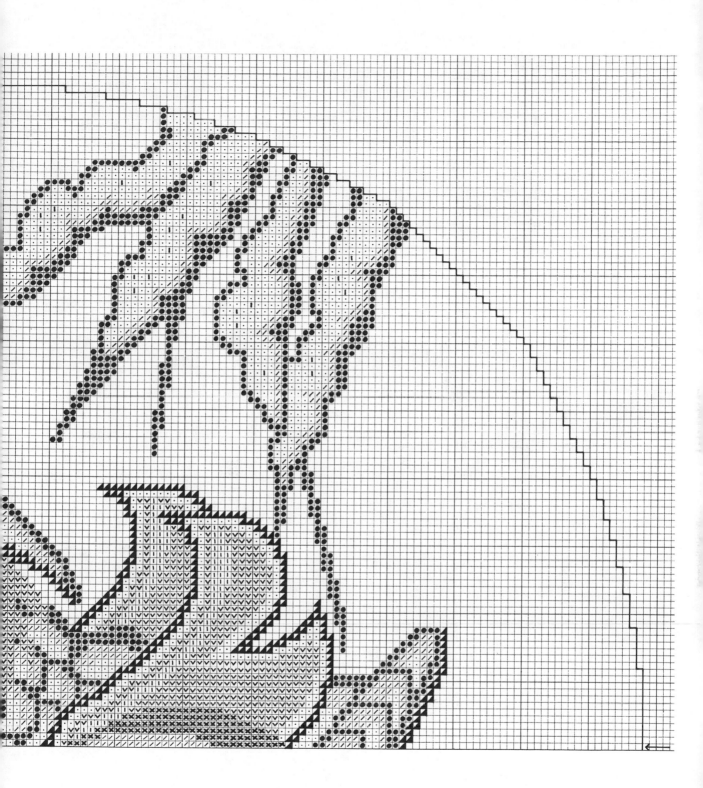

*Upper Right*

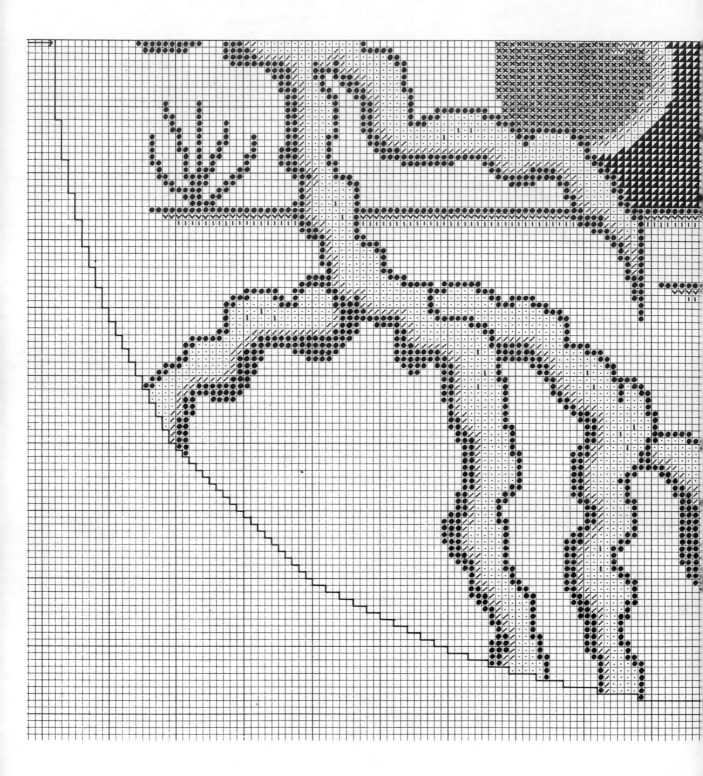

*Lower Left*

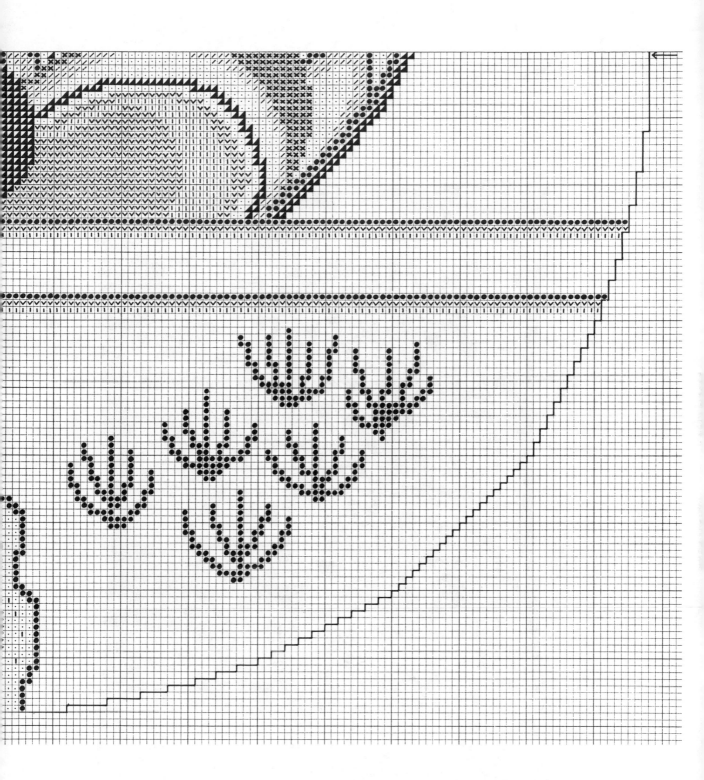

*Lower Right*

# JAPANESE EAGLE PILLOW

## History

The design for this pillow comes from a painting by Ito Jakuchu (1716–1800). The bold composition and brushwork do not seem like the work of an artist in the last year of a very long life. It has been suggested that Ito Jakuchu saw himself as the defiant eagle at the end of his life clinging to a snow-covered rock which slopes precipitously toward the churning and eternal sea below. The lack of many colors in this painting accentuates the somber scene.

## Canvas

The thread count for the design is 208 threads wide by 276 threads long.

If you choose 14 mesh canvas, cut and bind a piece of canvas 18 by 23 inches for a finished design approximately 15 by 20 inches.

If you choose 18 mesh canvas, cut and bind a piece of canvas 14½ by 18½ inches for a finished design approximately 11½ by 15½ inches.

## Stitching Directions

The graph is drawn in quarters—Upper Left, Upper Right, Lower Left, or Lower Right according to its position in relation to the whole design.

Follow the two arrows marked at the edges of each graph quarter until they intersect. This intersection marks the square on each quarter where you should begin stitching. Together, the four squares, one from each quarter, mark the center of the design.

Find and mark the center 4 meshes of your canvas with an indelible marker to correspond to the four center squares of the graph. From these center points, count outward and lightly mark the edges of the design on the canvas.

You are now ready to begin stitching. Counting from the center outward, stitch first the white out-lines of the eagle, then the brown outlines of the branch and lettering. Next fill in the brown areas of the eagle and then the white areas of the branch and lettering background. Finally, stitch the orange background.

## Color and Stitch Key

The background of the original painting was beige, which I changed to orange. Thread numbers refer to DMC pearl cotton. The location of the stitches used is noted on the key. The key instructs you to stitch the Tied Cross stitch variation background in orange and light orange. Referring to the Tied Cross stitch variation diagrams, work step 1 in light orange, steps 2 and 3 in orange, and step 4 in light orange. See Plate 3.

## Creative Alternatives

DESIGN CHANGES: Shorten the pillow by omitting the bottom portion of the branch on which the eagle rests. Cut off the pillow approximately 1½ inches below the bottom point of the eagle's tail.

Consider adding a border to the shortened version of the pillow. Add a 4-stitch dark brown border, then a 4-stitch white border, then a 16-stitch (or wider) dark brown border.

COLOR CHANGES: Replace the two-tone orange background with a two-tone light brown background of DMC pearl cotton (✳642 and ✳644).

Or stitch the eagle and branch in dark brown (✳938) and light brown (✳644); stitch the background in ecru.

STITCH CHANGES: Stitch the background in two-tone Double Cross stitch, Jacquard stitch variation, Oriental stitch, or St. George and St. Andrew Cross stitch.

If you add a border to the eagle, stitch the dark brown borders in Rhodes stitch over 4 meshes; stitch the white border in Slanting Gobelin stitch.

*Upper Left*

ORANGE #436, LIGHT ORANGE #738
TIED CROSS STITCH VARIATION

*Upper Right*

Lower Left

Lower Right

# JAPANESE WOODBLOCK
# PRINT PILLOW

## History

The design for this pillow comes from a woodblock print of an actor painted by Utagawa Toyokuni in 1807 at the height of the development of the multiple-produced color print. The Japanese painters had to keep in mind the inherent properties with which the engraver worked in chiseling the design into the woodblock. The designs, like the one here of an actor with large square sleeves, were consequently controlled with regard to the use of curves and lines and the distribution and combination of colors. Nonetheless, the painters were able to capture the spontaneity of actors, courtesans, and other inhabitants of the "floating world" in the pleasure quarters of Edo in the eighteenth and nineteenth centuries.

## Canvas

The thread count for the design is 200 threads wide by 260 threads long.

If you choose 14 mesh canvas, cut and bind a piece of canvas 17½ by 21½ inches for a finished design approximately 14½ by 18½ inches.

If you choose 18 mesh canvas, cut and bind a piece of canvas 14½ by 17½ inches for a finished design approximately 11½ by 14½ inches.

## Stitching Directions

The graph is drawn in quarters—Upper Left, Upper Right, Lower Left, or Lower Right according to its position in relation to the whole design.

Follow the two arrows marked at the edges of each graph quarter until they intersect. This intersection marks the square on each quarter where you should begin stitching. Together, the four squares, one from each quarter, mark the center of the design.

Find and mark the center 4 meshes of your canvas with an indelible marker to correspond to the four center squares of the graph. From these center points, count outward and lightly mark the border of the design on the canvas.

You are now ready to begin stitching. Counting from the center outward, stitch the face, the clothing outlines and details, the sword, and the lettering. Then fill in the clothing with Scotch stitch, and finally, the background with Woven stitch.

## Color and Stitch Key

The colors are similar to those in the original woodblock print. Yarn numbers refer to Paternayan yarn. The location of various stitches is noted on the key. See Plate 16.

## Creative Alternatives

DESIGN CHANGES:   For a smaller pillow, crop the design as in Figure 40.

*Figure 40*

COLOR CHANGES:   Change the color of the costume to blue (✳534 Paternayan yarn), green (✳603), or gold (✳742). If you choose blue or green, then change the neck and sword to orange (✳863) or gold.

STITCH CHANGES:   Stitch the costume in two-tone Double Cross stitch or in Rhodes stitch over 4 meshes. Stitch the sword in Continental or Basketweave; stitch the background in Jacquard stitch.

*Upper Left*

CHARCOAL GRAY #221

ORANGE #863
SCOTCH STITCH OVER 4 MESHES

ORANGE #863

BLUE #513

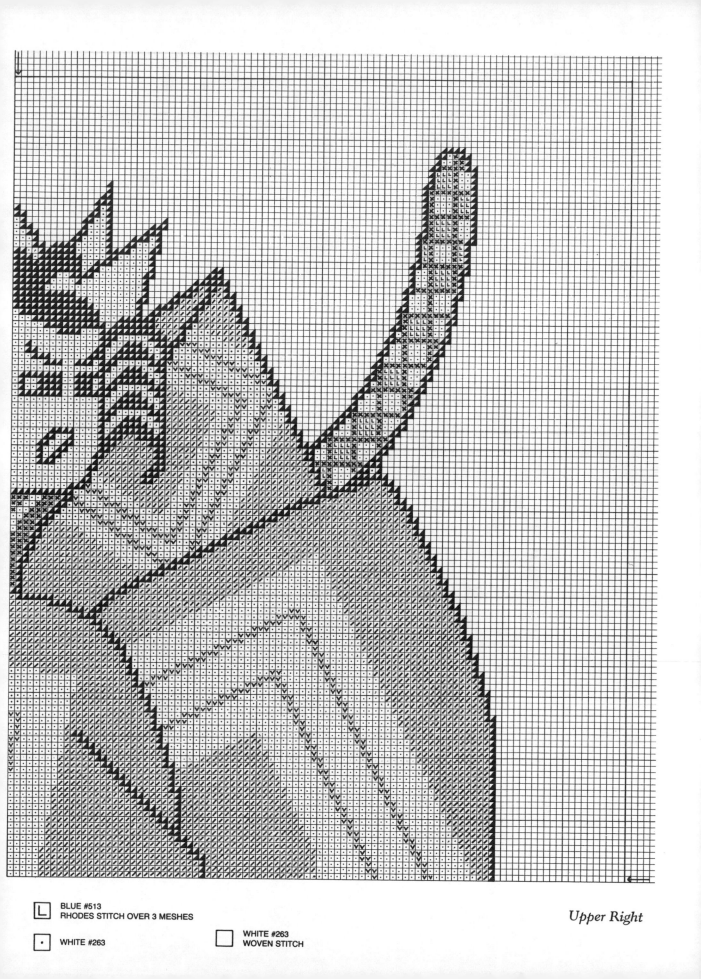

*Upper Right*

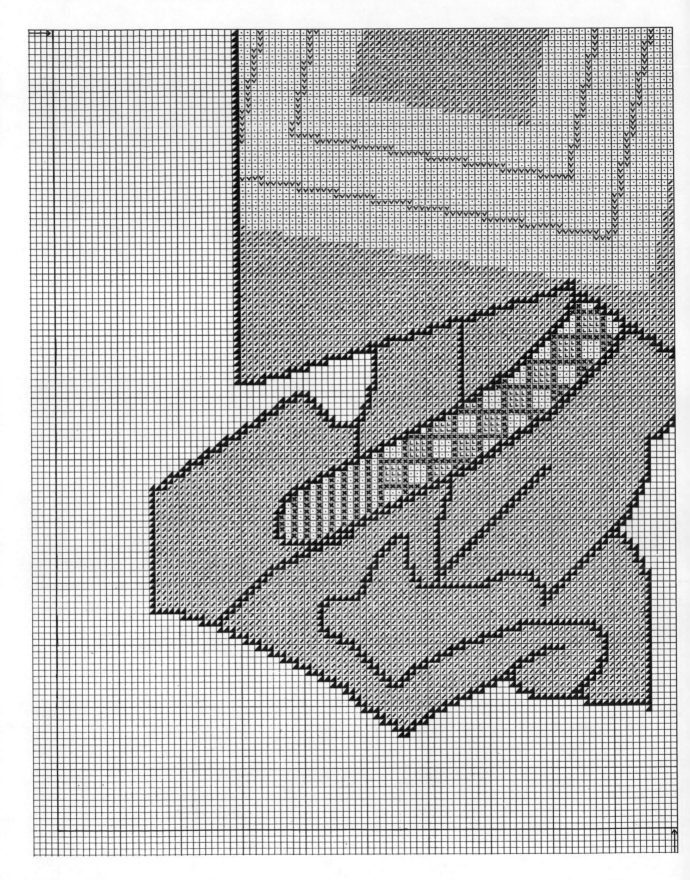

*Lower Left*

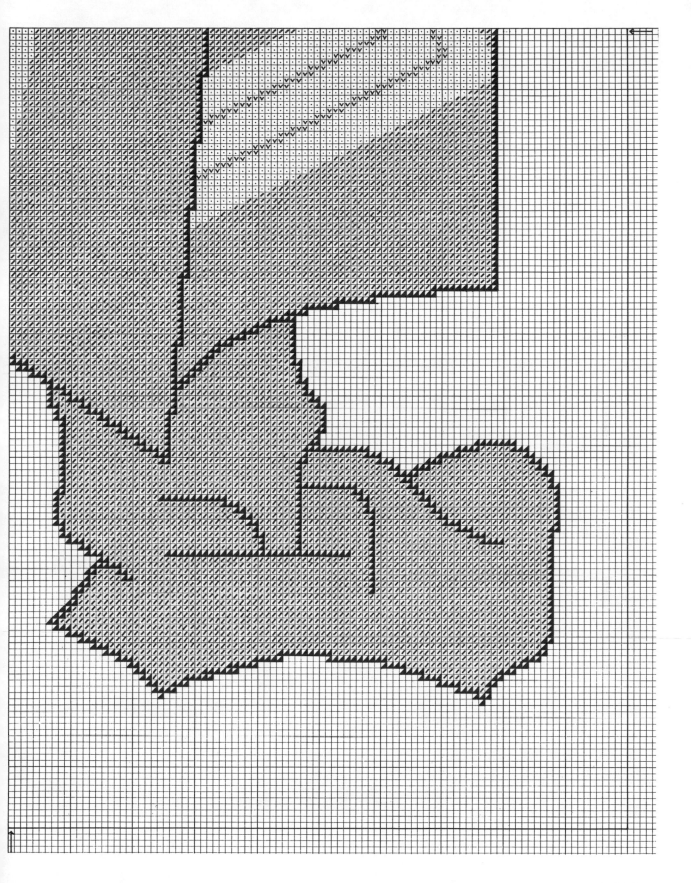

*Lower Right*

# DESIGNING YOUR OWN CANVASES

*North Persian Earthenware Pillow*

# DESIGNING

Traditional needlepoint (canvas embroidery) is basically a craft worked on a square canvas grid with yarn or thread to create a fabric. As a geometric craft, it has several limitations which can, however, be used to the advantage of the designs as well as to the integrity of the craft. The following chapters on designing your own canvases will help you understand some of the ways in which the limitations of geometric grid canvas can be used to enhance designs. They will also demonstrate the actual processes of planning and transferring designs to needlepoint canvas.

## The First Steps

Designs grow and evolve organically like plants rather than mechanically like machines. One idea will lead to another, which, in turn, leads to still others. One way to start designing your own canvases is to restitch a design already done. Make all those changes you wish had been there originally. Each of your changes will begin to make the design your own.

A good project for a beginning designer would be to change the Korean pincushion design in this book. Instead of stitching the pincushion in its modified diamond shape, add to the design sufficient background so that it becomes a rectangle, and then plan a border for the design. See Figures 41–45.

You might consider one of the following: Choose a decorative stitch and execute it with brown and white or blue-green and white. If you choose brown and white, incorporate blue-green as an accent color, working the color into the stitch pattern at

*Figure 41*

*Figure 42*

*Figure 43*

*Figure 44*

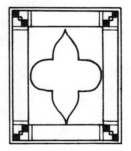

*Figure 45*

regular intervals. If you choose blue-green and white, incorporate brown as the accent color. Instead of using the accent color at regular intervals, you might decide to add it at irregular, random intervals. You could work the border in simple stripes, alternating the three colors and varying the widths of the stripes. Add to these stripes by developing blocks of color at each corner. You might stitch these blocks in Rhodes stitch or Waffle stitch.

You can change any of the design projects in this book by reading the creative alternatives listed for each design. Look at the designs as you read the creative alternatives and try to visualize not only the changes I have suggested but others that occur to you.

After you have embellished canvases designed by others, you may want to design your own canvases from the beginning. If you have never done any designing, your first step is to learn to observe design.

## Design Sources

The first step toward designing your own canvases is learning to observe the designs around you. Begin by looking for designs in your own household furnishings and in your garden. Search for designs in magazines and in the collections of current catalogues and cards. Collect swatches and clippings of designs and colors that appeal to you and store them in a drawer or box designated "design ideas."

Museums are excellent sources for designs. Take along a sketch pad or a camera with fast-speed film. Most museums have gift and book shops where you will find catalogues, posters, postcards, and greeting cards with good design ideas. The Japanese Woodblock Print pillow is a design I found in the Victoria and Albert Museum. The Korean Cranes pillow is a detail of a design from a Korean art traveling exhibition I saw in Seattle, Washington.

## Drawing Designs for Needlepoint Canvas

Gather together a few of your favorite clippings of designs, spread them out on a table, and try to visualize a simple needlepoint design from one clipping or from several in combination. The important thing is to find one aspect of a design with which to begin. Sketch your idea on a sheet of white bond paper. Keep an eraser nearby, and arrange and rearrange lines and shapes until the beginning of something pleasing is on your paper. Now stand back from your work and take a good look at your design. You may like one or two aspects of your drawing, but you may find several other parts you want to discard.

Trace on a sheet of tracing paper only the aspects of your sketch that you want to keep. Rework your traced design until you arrive at a simple design with just enough detail to please you and to do justice to the design. The emphasis here is on simplicity, as beginning needlepoint designers usually try to keep far too much detail in a drawing. It is often helpful to think of needlepoint designs in terms of a child's coloring book: the shapes are large, simple, and well defined.

To check whether your drawing has too much detail, use the test described in the section Choosing Canvas Mesh. Using this test, work and rework a drawing on tracing paper until you arrive at a design suitable for the canvas mesh you have chosen. Gradually you will learn how much detail various canvas sizes will allow.

Your drawing should be the same size as your finished needlepoint project. If you want to make a pillow 13 by 13 inches, you should make your drawing 13 by 13 inches. When you are satisfied with your sketch, draw a border around it. This will mark the edge of your finished project.

After you have sketched your first design for canvas, you may find it helpful to read about design theory. Discussions of line, space, rhythm, and balance may help you appraise and revise your design. Many embroiderers find Constance Howard's *Inspiration for Embroidery* (London: B. T. Batsford Ltd., 1971) and *Embroidery and Color* (New York: Van Nostrand Reinhold Co., 1976) of use in their work. Also take the opportunity to look at designs by your favorite designers. See how they handle different problems of design which trouble you. Each design presents its own set of problems and possibilities. The successful solution is most often a matter of drawing and redrawing.

It can also be helpful to do several design exercises. They should help you understand the flexibility inherent in the process of design at the same time that they force you to rethink the changes you make in your designs.

EXERCISE 1: Gather together ten sheets of bond paper approximately 6 by 8 inches or somewhat larger. On the first sheet draw a simple abstract design. On a second sheet redraw the first design, changing it. On a third sheet redraw the second design, again changing it. Repeat this process until you have ten drawings, each one with changes from the former. As you proceed, examine what each change does to the rhythm and balance of the design and note what you do to compensate for the changes.

EXERCISE 2: Gather four sheets of paper approximately 8 by 10 inches and one sheet of paper significantly larger. Draw a very small design on the first small sheet. On the second sheet, redraw the design, enlarging it. On the third sheet, redraw the design so that it now fills the paper. Place the fourth sheet on top of the larger sheet and redraw the design once more so that its boundaries flow off the fourth sheet and onto the larger sheet. Examine how the scale changes each of the drawings, and, in particular, what scale does to negative space.

Lift the fourth sheet off the larger sheet and compare the first and fourth designs to see what lack of boundary does to a design. I recently saw this used in a swim towel and suit. The swim towel was an appliqué of several colorful butterflies on a black background. The swimsuit was made of the design of one of the butterfly's wings, but without the outline of the wings. As such, it changed entirely, becoming an abstract design of veins unrelated to the butterfly.

As you work on designs for canvas, continue collecting design sources, reading about design theory, appraising the work of designers, and doing design exercises. All of these together will increase your visual awareness of design.

## Choosing Canvas Mesh

Once you have drawn a design that you want to transfer to canvas, decide which canvas mesh size is suitable for your design. The smaller the canvas mesh, the more details you can include in your design. For example, 18 mesh canvas will hold more details than 14 mesh canvas, and 14 mesh more

than 10 mesh. The smaller the canvas mesh, the more stitches per inch you have to indicate detail.

Eventually you will be able to predict fairly accurately the number of details possible for a given canvas mesh size. There is also a simple test that you may use: Darken the pencil lines of your drawing by tracing over them with a black felt-tip pen. Place a piece of canvas on top of your drawing and you will be able to see the darkened pen lines through the canvas. Study the drawing in relation to the canvas and imagine how you would stitch it. Ask yourself if the details will translate cleanly and effectively from a sketch to a piece of needlepoint. If your drawing is too detailed, try a finer canvas mesh, or trace the sketch again on tracing paper and rework the design, eliminating details that you cannot stitch. Keep on hand a sample piece of each size canvas mesh for just such tests.

When you study your first drawing in relation to canvas mesh size, you may find that you have too many details. If so, return to your drawing and eliminate many of the details. Check your work as you proceed by placing the canvas on top of the drawing. When you see that the canvas will allow you to stitch the remaining details, you will be ready to transfer your design to canvas.

## Transferring Your Design to Canvas

Find and mark the center of your drawing with a black felt-tip pen. At the same time, check your drawing to see that all pencil lines are darkened with a black felt-tip pen. Now cut a piece of canvas the size of your design plus a minimum of 3 inches in each direction for blocking and finishing.

Find the center of the canvas and mark it with an indelible marker. Place the canvas on top of your drawing, matching the center point of the canvas with the center point of the drawing.

Study the drawing in relation to the canvas; decide how you plan to stitch the canvas. Make certain that straight lines fall on the straight or cross grain of the canvas. If that is not possible, keep lines on the true diagonal of the canvas. If you plan to use decorative stitches, check that you have left sufficient space to allow the stitch pattern to develop.

As lightly as possible, trace the lines of your drawing onto the canvas with an indelible marker. Some designers tape the canvas on top of the drawing. If you do not tape the canvas, you can make small corrections in lines or shapes by twisting the canvas slightly in one direction or another as you trace.

Once you have traced the design onto the canvas, you are ready to begin stitching. If you want to paint your canvas before stitching, see the section on Painting Canvases.

## The Advantages of a Graphed Design

Transferring a design directly from a freehand drawing onto canvas is most suitable for non-repeating, free-flowing designs with a minimum number of details. If you have sketched a complex design with repeating or mirror-image patterns, you will want to graph your drawing and then count it onto canvas. By doing a graph, you can plan repeating patterns so that they repeat with precisely the same number of stitches. For examples, see the Korean Cranes pillow and the Persian glasses case. All motifs repeat exactly at precise intervals.

A counted and graphed mirror-image design means that one half of the design will be exactly the same as the second half. For examples, see the East Persian Lions pillow and the Tibetan purse.

By counting a graphed four-way design, each quarter will be equal, stitch by stitch, to the others. For examples, see the Persian rug and the Japanese Imari pillow.

Graphing a design helps you plan balanced decorative stitch units so that the project incorporates whole stitch units wherever possible. For an example, see the Persian Rose and Nightingale pillow. The border is balanced so that whole stitch units of Rhodes stitch and Scotch stitch are used.

Even if there are no repeat patterns, graphing a drawing makes it easier to work out the intricacies of design details by planning ahead the correct number of threads necessary for stitching those details. They can be worked and reworked until they are ready for stitching. See, for example, the blue and white crisscross pattern in the Japanese Imari pillow; or the patterns on the clothing, saddles, and blankets on the Persian Falconer and Persian Hunter pillows.

Graphing also makes possible proper outlines and well-constructed curves and circles. These techniques are discussed in the sections on lines and outlines, curves, and circles.

## Thread Count

In the section on Canvas under General Instructions, I discuss the thread count of a design and how you use it as part of a formula for calculating the size requirements of graphed designs on various canvas meshes. When you begin designing graphs, thread count again becomes important.

Two examples using thread count in planning graphs follow: Imagine a footstool for which you need to stitch a design 16 by 12 inches on 14 mesh canvas. How large must you make your graph on 10-to-the-inch graph paper for a finished project 16 by 12 inches on 14 mesh canvas? First, find the thread count for the prospective design by multiplying the size in inches by the size of the canvas mesh:

16 (width in inches) by 14 (canvas mesh size) = 224 thread count

12 (length in inches) by 14 (canvas mesh size) = 168 thread count

Next, divide the thread count of the design by the graph paper grid size to find the size the project should be on graph paper:

224 (thread count) ÷ 10 (graph paper grid size) = 22.4 inches

168 (thread count) ÷ 10 (graph paper grid size) = 16.8 inches

You must, therefore, plan a design 22.4 by 16.8 inches on 10 grid graph paper for a finished project 16 by 12 inches on 14 mesh canvas.

Suppose you have drawn a graphed design measuring 13 by 15 inches on 10 grid graph paper and you want to know how large a piece of 18 mesh canvas you need to stitch the design. First, multiply the size of the design in inches by the size of the graph paper grid to find the thread count:

13 (project width in inches) by 10 (graph paper grid) = 130 thread count

15 (project length in inches) by 10 (graph paper grid) = 150 thread count

Next, divide the thread count by the size of the canvas mesh to determine the size of the project in inches:

130 (thread count) ÷ 18 (canvas mesh) = 7¼ inches project width

150 (thread count) ÷ 18 (canvas mesh) = 8⅓ inches project length

Thus the size of your finished project will be 7¼ by 8⅓ inches on 18 mesh canvas.

## Transferring a Drawing to Graph Paper

If you sketch a design and transfer it to graph paper, you can proceed in two different ways. Draw your design on white drawing paper, working and reworking it as noted in the section on drawing designs for needlepoint canvas. Graph paper is now available in grid sizes that correspond to canvas mesh sizes. Choose a graph paper grid using the same criteria noted in the section on choosing a canvas mesh size. Using pencil, lightly trace your design onto graph paper. See Figure 46.

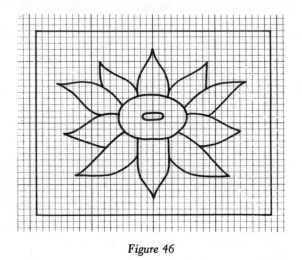

*Figure 46*

The other way to proceed is to decide approximately how large you want your finished project to be and what canvas mesh size you plan to use. Calculate the approximate thread count (see Thread Count) and outline the size of your project on 10-to-the-inch graph paper. Trace a corresponding border on white drawing paper and sketch your design as noted in the section on drawing designs for needlepoint canvas. When your drawing is finished, trace it lightly in pencil onto 10-to-the-inch graph paper. See Figure 46. For example, if you plan to

work a project 12 by 12 inches on 14 mesh canvas, sketch a design approximately 17 by 17 inches and transfer it to 10-to-the-inch graph paper.

Now that your drawing is lightly traced onto graph paper, begin blocking in your design by marking those squares adjacent to your sketch. Each graph square will represent 1 needlepoint stitch. See Figure 47.

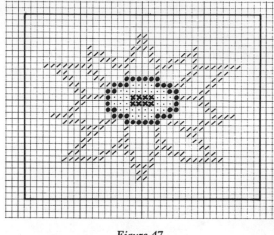

*Figure 47*

## Lines and Outlines

If you look carefully at outlines on a stitched canvas, you will find that you can divide them into three categories: 1) outlines on the straight grain or cross grain of the canvas; 2) outlines on the true diagonal of the canvas; 3) outlines falling off the straight grain, cross grain, or true diagonal. Stitched as separate lines, each of the above will be straight. Needlepoint curves are formed by joining segments of these straight lines to create the illusion of a curve.

Outlines on the straight or cross grain of the canvas are stitched easily, one stitch directly below another stitch, forming a vertical row, or one stitch directly beside another stitch, forming a horizontal row. Such outlines are tidy, consistent, unbroken lines.

Outlines on the true diagonal (bias) of the canvas can be stitched in two directions, from upper right to lower left and from upper left to lower right. If you stitch diagonal outlines as most stitchers do, you will make them one stitch diagonally below another stitch, forming a single row in imitation of the single-row outline stitch on the straight or cross grain. See Figure 48. Compare the diagonal outlines with the straight and cross grain outlines. The stitches of the diagonal row from upper right to lower left appear connected because each single tent stitch lies on the canvas from upper

broken stitches, a somewhat better solution, but still not satisfactory. A better solution is to stitch a double line instead of a single line. By stitching a second row, your diagonal outline is now a series of 2-stitch horizontal and vertical lines: 1 stitch below the first, 1 stitch beside the second, 1 stitch below the next, 1 stitch beside the next, and so on. Besides connecting the stitches and giving your outline an unbroken appearance, the second row also adds to the thickness of the outline, making it resemble more closely the straight and cross grain outlines. See Figure 49.

Once you have doubled the diagonal outline from upper left to lower right, compare it with the single diagonal line from upper right to lower left. The latter is now not only thinner than the straight and cross grain outlines, but much thinner than the upper left to lower right diagonal line. To make it more equal in proportion to the other outlines, dou-

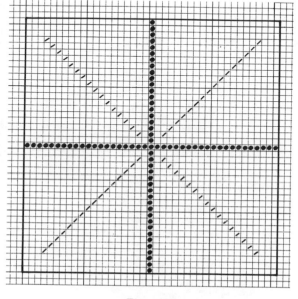

*Figure 48*

right to lower left, but the whole row appears much thinner than its straight or cross grain counterpart.

When you compare the diagonal outline from upper left to lower right with the straight and cross grain outlines, you will see that it does not look like a smooth line. Rather, it appears as a series of un-joined single stitches, which may be annoying as your eye jumps from stitch to stitch instead of moving smoothly over the outline. This is because the direction of each single tent stitch, from upper right to lower left, lies at odds with the direction of the outline from upper left to lower right.

Stitchers, who are bothered by the broken line, have devised methods to make the stitches of the outline appear connected. Some have reversed the direction of the tent stitches. This is not recommended because the stitches should lie in the same direction. Other stitchers tramé under the line of

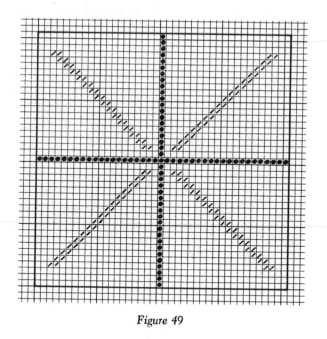

*Figure 49*

ble it from 1 row to 2 rows. Although it will be slightly thicker than the straight and cross grain outlines, it will nonetheless resemble all outlines more closely than it did as a single row.

When you are planning straight lines, keep your lines on the straight or cross grain of the canvas wherever possible. For example, see the blue and white crisscross section of the Japanese Imari pillow. Here I have kept all single lines on the straight and cross grain of the canvas even though such lines go in other directions on original Imari plates and platters. See the Persian Elephants pillow with its small charcoal and purple lines on the elephants' trunks. I have kept these small 3-to-6-stitch lines purposely on the straight and cross grain of the canvas. They are much straighter, cleaner, and more consistent than they would be had I tried to make them graduate along the diagonal from vertical to horizontal in such a limited space.

If you cannot keep lines on the straight or cross grain of the canvas, your next best choice is the true diagonal of the canvas. See the four diagonal black feather outlines in the Persian Rose and Nightingale pillow. See also the cranes' bills in the Korean Cranes pillow.

If neither of the above is possible, you must use lines that fall off the straight grain, cross grain, or diagonal. These lines, which I call "off-grain" lines, take a bit more planning than the others since they look best when you plan them in graduated steps.

In Figure 50 I have drawn a few off-grain lines on graph paper. If you were to transfer these lines to canvas and stitch them, you would choose at random which mesh to stitch, your only criterion being that the black ink of the marker touches the mesh. Consequently you might have stitched lines similar to those in Figure 51. Now compare the lines in Figure 51 with the lines in Figure 52. Both sets of lines represent the same angles, but notice the difference: the lines in Figure 52 graduate at precisely planned intervals, making them straighter than the random lines. For example, the pattern established by the top line in Figure 52 is a series of 3 horizontal stitches. Note the relationship of the third stitch of the first 3 stitches and the first stitch of the second 3 stitches. One is directly vertical to the other. I planned this vertical step so that the line remains unbroken and as consistent in thickness as possible. Had I made this a diagonal rather than a vertical relationship, and then incorporated the pattern into a mirror-image design, the line from the upper left to lower right would appear broken, just as a single row on the true diagonal from upper left to lower right appears broken.

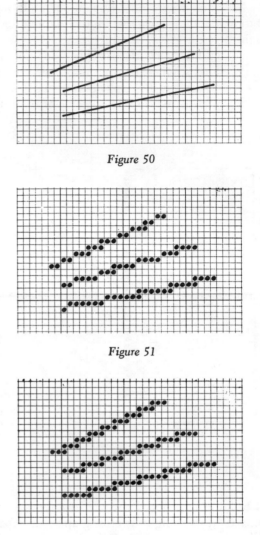

Figure 50

Figure 51

Figure 52

The other patterns established in Figure 52 are 4 horizontal stitches and 5 horizontal stitches. These happen to be patterns of horizontal stitches. In Figure 53 I have graphed straight grain, cross grain, and diagonal lines and then added off-grain lines to show the relationship of off-grain line patterns to the straight grain, cross grain, and diagonal lines. Note when the patterns are horizontal and when they are vertical. Note also that the pattern of stitches for off-grain lines increases in number of stitches as the angle of the off-grain line changes from the diagonal to the straight or cross grain.

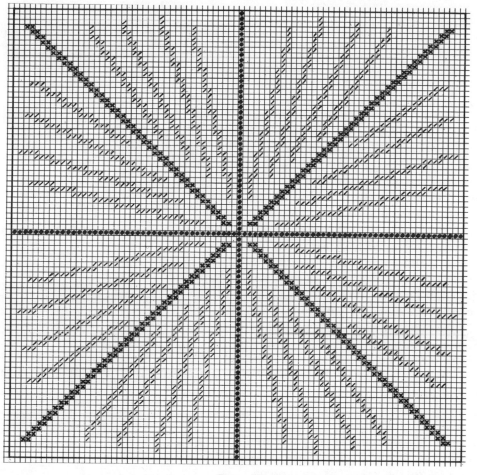

*Figure 53*

These relationships become more important when you begin constructing curves and circles.

The above diagrams of off-grain lines show you but a few of the patterns of off-grain lines. Depending on the angle of the line, the patterns can be 2 stitches, 3 stitches, 4, 5, 6, 7, or 8 stitches, or any combination of these, such as 2-3-2-3 or 6-6-7-6-6-7. To decide the pattern, sketch the line on graph paper, then with pencil try out a number of patterns until you find the pattern that best follows your line. It is not important which pattern you decide to use, only that you follow the pattern so that you have a tidy, straight line, consistent in its graduating steps. For examples of stitched off-grain line patterns, see the orange and white blocks on the Kabuki actor's sleeves in the Japanese Woodblock Print pillow. The orange off-grain lines are horizontal patterns of 7 stitches (left block) and 3 stitches

(right block). The vertical patterns are 6 stitches (left block) and 3 stitches (right block). See also the hunter's bow and arrow in the Persian Hunter pillow. The top string of the bow is a horizontal pattern of 4 stitches; the arrow is also a horizontal pattern of 4 stitches. The bottom string of the bow is a line on the true diagonal.

At this point you may wonder how these comments apply to shapes with no outlines. Wherever the edge of a shape is straight, you should use the same guidelines you use for outlines. Stay on the straight or cross grain of the canvas. If that is not possible, keep the edge of a shape on the true diagonal. If that is impossible and you decide to use an off-grain line, find a consistently graduated pattern of stitches. For examples, see the garments, saddles, blankets, and horses' legs in the Persian Hunter and Persian Falconer pillows.

## Curves

If you were to draw a gentle curve on canvas, such as the one in Figure 54, and stitch it, you would likely follow your pen line, stitching the meshes marked with black ink, and your curve might be similar to the one in Figure 55. If you compare the curve in Figure 55 with the curve in Figure 56, you will see that the former is stitched at random, guided only by the pen line, while the latter is stitched following a definite pattern established by increasing or decreasing the number of stitches in a row.

Constructing curves is similar to constructing off-grain lines in one respect: you must determine a pattern for successive rows. The process differs, however, in one important respect. Off-grain lines are made up of a consistent number of stitches forming a straight line, for example a horizontal pattern of 5-5-5-5 as in Figure 52. A curve is made by decreasing the number of stitches in each row as in A in Figure 57, or increasing the number of stitches in each row as in B in Figure 57.

Look closely at the relationship of the row of 5 stitches to the next row of 4 stitches in A in Figure 57. Note the relationship of the fifth (last) stitch in the row of 5 to the first stitch in the row of 4. One is directly horizontal to the other. As in the construction of off-grain outlines, I planned this horizontal step so that the outline remains unbroken.

At this point, look back at Figure 53 and again study the relationship of off-grain line patterns to

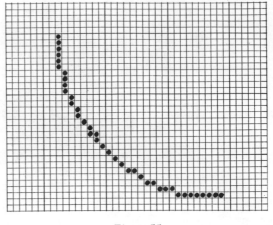

*Figure 55*

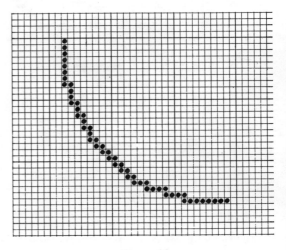

*Figure 56*

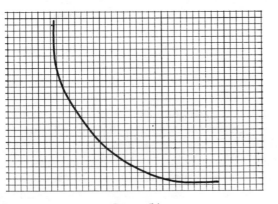

*Figure 54*

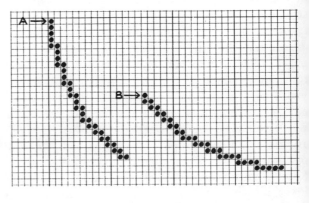

*Figure 57*

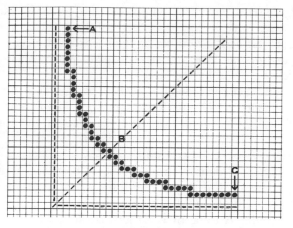

*Figure 58*

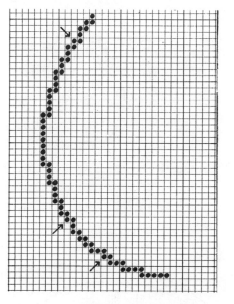

*Figure 60*

straight grain, cross grain, and diagonal lines. Note that the number of stitches forming patterns for off-grain lines changes as the angle of the off-grain line changes. The closer the angle is to the diagonal, the shorter the number of stitches in the off-grain pattern. The closer the angle is to the straight or cross grain lines, the longer the number of stitches in the off-grain line pattern.

In Figure 58, I have drawn a curve and marked the diagonal line and the straight and cross grain lines. Note how the pattern creating the curve develops from point A (the straight grain of the canvas) to point B (the diagonal line of the canvas) and from point B to point C (the cross grain of the canvas). From point A to point B the curve pattern is a series of decreases, 8-5-4-3-3-2-2. From point B to point C the curve pattern is a series of increases. Whenever a curve moves from the straight or cross grain toward the diagonal line of the canvas, the stitch pattern will decrease.

In Figure 59, you will see curves of varying patterns. How sharply or gradually the pattern of a curve increases or decreases depends on how sharply or gradually a curve is drawn. The important factor is not the curve pattern you choose, but that you always decrease from the straight or cross grain to the diagonal and always increase from the diagonal to the straight or cross grain.

The one exception to this occurs when you move from patterns of 3-3-3 to patterns of 2-2-2 (the diagonal). Here the change may often be too sharp. If so, you may want to temporize with a pattern of 2-3-2-3 between the pattern of 3-3-3 and 2-2-2. See Figure 60.

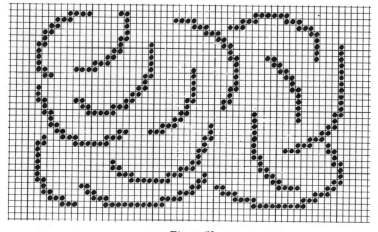

*Figure 59*

189

For examples of outline curves, see the Japanese Eagle pillow, the Chinese Rose Medallion pillow, the Korean Tortoise and Snake pillow, and the Chinese Butterflies bell pull.

For examples of curves in shapes with no outlines, see the Japanese Mandarin Duck pillow, the Persian Elephants pillow, the Persian Hunter and Persian Falconer pillows, and the Chinese Garden bell pull.

## Circles

Constructing a circle employs many of the same principles as constructing a curve. Rather than drawing a circle at random and hoping it looks round when you have stitched it, you must plan the circle, making decreases and increases at consistent intervals so that the resulting circle is as round as stitch patterns allow.

Begin by marking a center point on graph paper with a pencil. Use the intersection of 2 lines as a center point. (You will ultimately use the four squares around the intersection as four centers, one belonging to each circle quarter. See Planning for Decorative Stitches.)

Decide how large the circle will be, and measure the radius from the center point to the circle's edge. Place the 1-inch mark of a ruler on the center point and slowly rotate the ruler, marking the edge of the circle as in Figure 61. When you have marked the entire circle, recheck the accuracy of your markings. Mark with an X the four center squares around the center point. Mark with an X each straight and cross grain line radiating out from the four center squares. Next, mark the diagonal lines radiating out from the center squares. See Figure 62.

Begin with the top square marked A. Moving clockwise toward point B, block in the squares following your pencil lines and forming a pattern by decreasing the number of stitches in each row, just as you would construct a curve. See Figure 63.

When you have blocked in the edge from A to B, examine the pattern, in this case 6-4-3-3-2-2. You will use this same pattern to block in the rest of the circle. Moving from B to C, reverse the pattern so that it forms a mirror image of the A to B pattern. From D to E, reverse the pattern again, and again from E to F. Repeat the pattern, reversing it each one eighth until you have blocked in the circle. See

Figure 64. If you have completed this correctly, the patterns on all four quarters will be exactly the same, just as the number of squares from the center points to the cross and straight grain points on the circle edge will be the same.

Construct each circle, regardless of its size, in the same manner. The pattern established in Figure 64 will change as the size of the circle changes, but the procedure remains the same. Figure 65 shows a series of blocked-in concentric circles.

Since the pattern from point A to point B is repeated all the way around the circle, you may wonder why it would not be better to measure only from point A to point B rather than to draw all the way around the circle as in Figure 62. If you mea-

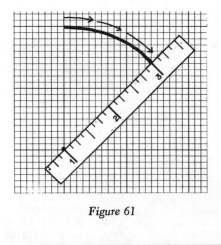

*Figure 61*

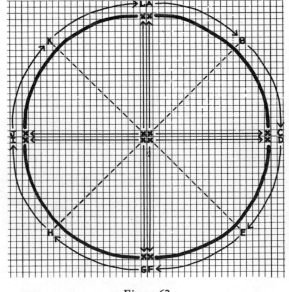

*Figure 62*

190

sure only from A to B, you may block in your whole circle only to discover that the circle has slight "peaks."

If you plan to stitch the circle as an outline, be certain to connect each row of stitches by placing the first stitch of each succeeding row directly vertically or horizontally to the last stitch of the row before. If you make this a diagonal rather than a horizontal or vertical relationship, the line of the circle from points D to F and from points J to L will appear broken.

For examples of circles, see the Korean Cranes pillow. Each of the five cranes is surrounded by two circles. One is a brown outline, the other is a white band. The pattern for the brown-outline circle from

point A to point B is 7-4-4-3-3-3-2-2-2-2. The pattern for the outer edge of the white circle from point A to point B is 7-4-4-4-3-3-3-2-2-2-2.

See also the North Persian Earthenware pillow. There are charcoal gray outlines around the fish and on either side of the script. The pattern for the first charcoal gray outline around the fish from point A to point B is 9-5-4-3-3-2-3-2-2-2.

## Choosing Decorative Stitches

To use decorative stitches effectively, you must plan designs with shapes simple and large enough to accommodate stitch patterns without producing an overall effect that is choppy and confusing. See, for example, the Persian Rose and Nightingale pillow or the Japanese Woodblock Print pillow. Several of the design areas in those pillows are large enough to accommodate decorative stitches. By contrast, see the Japanese Imari pillow or the Chinese Rose Medallion pillow. Here the designs are sufficiently detailed that there is essentially no room for decorative stitches. Adding even the simplest decorative stitch will only add confusion to an already busy design. Use texture with a degree of restraint. Often the use of too many decorative stitches in a single project will detract from the overall impact of the design. It is not possible to devise exact rules for using texture, as each design presents its own possibilities. It is prudent when choosing decorative stitches to err on the side of too few rather than too many stitches.

When choosing decorative stitches, keep in mind the scale of the stitch. Use a large-scale stitch, such as Tile stitch, only in an area large enough for the stitch pattern to develop. See the Korean Tortoise and Snake pillow. Here is a background area large enough for the full development of the stitch. A large-scale stitch in a small area will make a choppy effect. For example, Tile stitch would not work well as a background stitch for the Korean Cranes pillow because the background consists only of smaller areas with no large spaces.

Finally, when choosing several stitches for a project, choose a variety of scales. For example, in the Japanese Woodblock Print pillow, the scale of the Scotch stitch for the costume is significantly larger than the Woven stitch of the background.

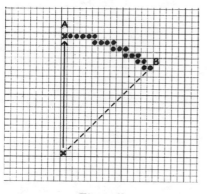

Figure 63

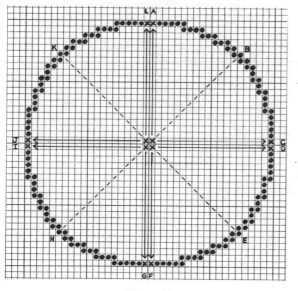

Figure 64

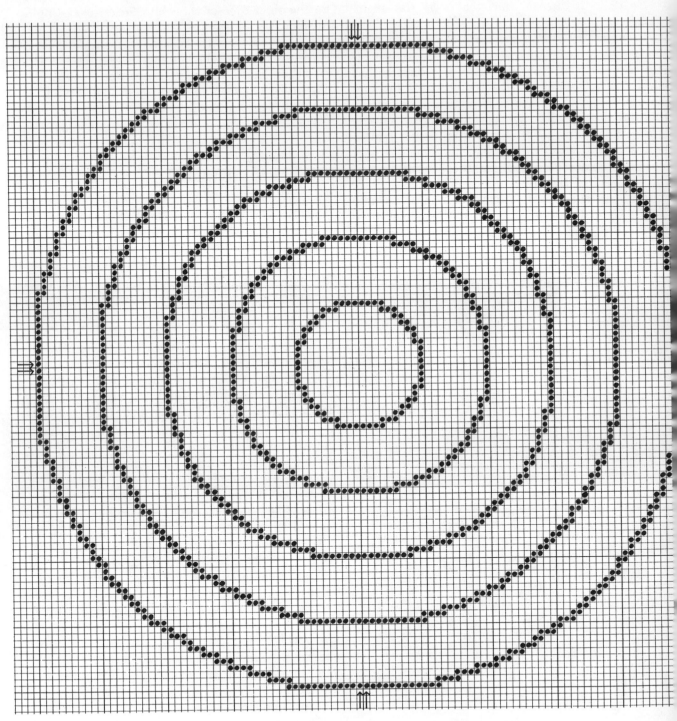

Figure 65

## Planning for Decorative Stitches

Throughout the instructions and explanations for designing your own canvases, you will notice that a single center point is a rarity. More likely, you will find references to four center canvas meshes or graph squares. The reason for this has to do with the use of decorative stitches.

A great number of decorative stitches, particularly Block, Cross, or Tied stitches, are worked over even numbers of canvas meshes. The pattern for Scotch stitch, for example, is most commonly worked over 4 meshes. If you plan a single-center canvas mesh rather than double-center meshes the thread count will be an odd number of threads, rather than an even number. Since Scotch stitch over 4 meshes uses an even number of threads, the last Scotch stitch unit in a row of Scotch stitches will be over an odd number of threads, thus differing from the other stitch units by plus or minus 1 thread. See Figure 66.

If you use 2 center meshes instead of 1, the thread count is even and the number of Scotch stitches becomes 3 complete units to the left and 3 complete units to the right. See Figure 67.

Figures 66 and 67 pertain to horizontal thread count. The same problems also occur with vertical thread count. With a single center, as in Figure 68, the thread count will be uneven and the bottom Scotch stitch unit is worked over 3 threads rather than 4. If you use 2 center meshes instead of only 1, the thread count will be even and the number of Scotch stitches becomes 3 complete units to the top

and 3 complete units to the bottom as in Figure 69.

If you put together the 2 horizontal center meshes and the 2 vertical center meshes, you will understand the necessity for 4 center meshes, one belonging to each quarter of the entire design. Figure 70 uses 4 center meshes, allowing 36 complete units of Scotch stitch radiating evenly outward from the center meshes.

Contrast this diagram with Figure 71, which uses

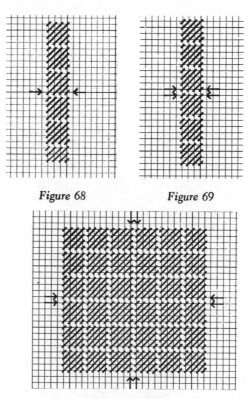

Figure 68          Figure 69

Figure 70

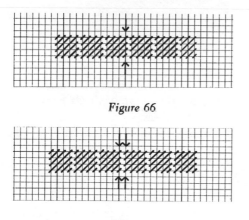

Figure 66

Figure 67

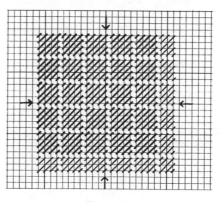

Figure 71

193

only 1 center mesh. Here the Scotch stitch units along the right and bottom sides are worked over 3 by 4 meshes instead of 4 by 4 meshes, and the unit at the bottom right corner over 3 by 3 meshes.

You might think this process unnecessary if you simply added a fourth mesh along the right and bottom edges of Figure 71, thereby making the Scotch stitch units 4 by 4 meshes instead of 3 by 4 meshes. As a result, you would question the need for planning ahead and using 4 center meshes instead of 1. This is possible with Figure 71, but not if you had planned and stitched a border around a design from a single center point, and then planned to use Scotch stitch as a background. You would then find yourself in a situation similar to Figure 72. You would be plus or minus 1 thread and thus not able to complete the right and bottom Scotch stitches over 4 by 4 meshes. Since you had already stitched the border, you would not have the option of adding or subtracting a single thread without unbalancing the border.

If you planned and stitched a 2- or 4-way design and chose Scotch stitch as a background, you would want the stitch units on either side, top, and bottom to be identically balanced around the design as in Figure 73. Compare this diagram with Figure 72, where the design is counted and stitched from a single center mesh.

If by chance you found yourself in one of the situations I have described, you might ask why you could not change the scale of Scotch stitch from 4 meshes, an even count, to 3 meshes, an odd count. You can rescale Scotch stitch but other stitches often cannot be rescaled. Moreover, if you use 4 center meshes you can choose which scale of Scotch stitch you want to use over 3 meshes, 4, 5, or 6. Compare Figure 74, illustrating Scotch stitch over 3 meshes, with Figure 70. Both use 4 center meshes.

If you know from the outset of your project that you will use a stitch worked over an odd number of threads, then you can plan your design to use an odd thread count.

Another point is important in planning decorative stitches: the number of meshes each stitch unit incorporates. Scotch stitch is most commonly stitched over 4 meshes. If you want to use Scotch stitch over 4 meshes in a certain area of your design, you should plan that area in combinations of 4 meshes to incorporate total units of Scotch stitch.

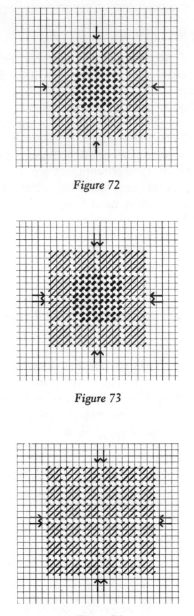

Figure 72

Figure 73

Figure 74

See, for example, the Scotch stitch border of the Persian Elephants pillow.

If you have not decided which stitches you will use in a given design, plan areas of 12 meshes which make it possible to use a great number of stitches worked over 2, 3, 4, or 6 meshes. If you plan areas in combinations of 24 meshes, you will be able to use those stitches as well as those worked over meshes.

For examples of areas planned for total stitch units, see the Persian Elephants pillow, the Persian Rose and Nightingale pillow, the Indian Egg pillow, and the borders for the Persian Hunter and Persian Falconer pillows.

## Choosing Colors

A theoretical understanding of color is helpful to the designer. Constance Howard's *Embroidery and Color* (New York: Van Nostrand Reinhold Co., 1976) is a good basic source for the study of color applied to needlework.

You can also begin your study of color with a collection of scraps of colors and color combinations you find appealing. Cut squares of cardboard and wrap leftover yarns and threads around each square, one color per square. When you have collected a diverse selection of color squares, combine and recombine several, constantly changing the combinations by adding and subtracting hues and values. When you find combinations that appeal to you, make note of them. Keep adding new squares to your collection and use them as an ongoing study, experimenting with still other combinations.

Place several squares of color on a large black surface such as a black matte board and examine what effect the black has upon the color squares. Shift the same squares to a large white surface and notice the different effect.

Search through magazines and catalogues for interesting color combinations; clip the examples and keep a notebook of them. Use your notebook as an ongoing source of color, adding to it as possible.

Color preference is personal but as you experiment with color combinations, you will discover several universal qualities of color. One color changes the perception of another, which in turn influences others. Combine, for example, a favorite blue with three values of a favorite green and you may discover that the blue kills the greens and all take on a slightly sick look. Choose, however, another blue and suddenly the greens come alive and the new blue becomes an entirely different color. Even after you have found appealing combinations of blue and green, continue to experiment. You may end with three values of blue and one green, all four values entirely different from your original choices. Color

has an elusive way of choosing its own partners, so approach color choice with flexibility.

Most people have a favorite color and also a color they dislike. Choose your least favorite color, one you usually avoid if possible, and concentrate on it. Use it in a series of color combinations, organizing and reorganizing colors around it until you find it pleasing. This exercise is one of my favorite because it demonstrates that one color rarely stands alone uninfluenced by the context of other colors.

Proportion also plays an important role in color selection. A vast amount of rust added to the blue-green color combination mentioned above may overwhelm the blue and green values. But a rust accent may add interest to all the colors.

Look critically at the colors you have used in past needlework projects and ask yourself if the colors remain fresh to your eye. If yes, decide what you admire about them. If not, decide by color experiments what you would do to change them if you were to restitch them. This may help you with future color choices.

When you are ready to choose colors for a project, select all of your colors at one time. Gather them together in a group and examine the effect of each on the others. Try to guess the proportions you will need. If you plan to use only a few strands of red as an accent color, do not add 4 ounces of red yarn to your color grouping.

Often a group of yarns gathered together will look different from the same group partially stitched on a canvas. You might stitch a bit of each color yarn in an appropriate place on your canvas. Looking from the stitched samples to the group of yarns, try to visualize how the colors will look on a stitched canvas. A stitched strand of yarn looks darker than an unstitched strand. This is because the edges of each stitch fall in the shadow of the stitches beside it.

You may find it helpful to paint a preliminary sketch of your canvas, adjusting and readjusting the placement of colors. Even though you have a painted guide, you may change your mind as you choose yarns and threads. The texture of yarn influences the light reflection in such a way that the same color in yarn and paint will be quite different. Look on a painted guide as only a preliminary step toward color choice. Make your final decisions when you see the yarns or threads.

## Painting Canvases

Painting a needlepoint canvas is an optional step. You can stitch a design simply by counting from a graph or by tracing the design outlines lightly on canvas. Painting a canvas has some advantage. It provides a background of the same color beneath the yarn. This prevents flecks of light canvas from showing through your stitching if the yarn does not cover the canvas threads perfectly. The painted colors also serve as a guide for placement of the yarns you have chosen.

Supplies necessary for painting canvases include paints, brushes, a palette, a jar for water, and one or two paper towels for blotting brushes. Types of paints and brushes are listed in the section on supplies.

There are two ways to proceed in painting a canvas. First, trace lightly the outlines of the design onto the canvas with an indelible marker, and then paint the design with the colors you have chosen. The second method eliminates tracing the outlines of the design onto the canvas. Place the canvas on top of your drawing, and using the outlines of the drawing underneath the canvas as a guide, paint the design with the colors you have chosen.

Many designers tape the canvas on top of the design to secure it in place. I prefer to have the canvas loose on top of the drawing so that I can shift the canvas to adjust and correct certain lines and shapes to follow the canvas grain. If you feel the need to hold your canvas in place, use a couple of paperweights. They will secure your canvas but you can still shift it easily to make corrections.

Painting a canvas is easier if you thin the paint to the proper consistency so that it spreads evenly on the canvas, yet is not so thick as to clog the canvas holes. Begin by thinning the paint to the consistency of heavy cream and then adjust as necessary. If paint does clog the canvas holes, blot the paint with a paper towel or a dry brush.

When you mix paints, remember that the paint color will dry darker and duller on canvas than on a wet palette.

# FINISHING THE PROJECT

# FINISHING

## Professional Finishing

Once you have completed the stitching part of your project, you must block it and then make it into its final form as a pillow or whatever. This you can do yourself, if you are an accomplished seamstress, or you may want to have a professional needlepoint finisher do the work for you. Needlepoint is time-consuming and it would be foolish to ruin a piece of work with careless finishing.

If you decide to use a professional finisher, check his reputation before you leave your work with him. Ask to see several projects he has finished.

If you decide to do your own finishing, I suggest you also consult one of the books on needlepoint finishing currently on the market. It will augment my more general instructions.

## Blocking

Blocking should smooth and set the yarn. If you did not use a frame for stitching your project, blocking will restore your canvas to its original shape.

To block a piece of needlepoint, you need the following supplies: a plywood board larger than your project, brass brads and a hammer or a staple gun, a T square, brown wrapping paper approximately the size of the plywood board, and a waterproof marking pen.

STEP 1: Measure the size of your needlepoint project. Use a T square to make the lines perpendicular and the corners square and then draw an outline of the project on brown wrapping paper with a waterproof pen. Secure the wrapping paper to the plywood board.

STEP 2: Wrap the dry piece of needlepoint in a wet, lukewarm bath towel and leave it for several hours until it is quite damp but not soaked.

STEP 3: Remove the needlepoint from the towel and tack it face up on the paper with brass brads or a staple gun at 1-inch intervals so that the stitched design conforms to the outline marked on the paper. Leave the canvas on the board until it is completely dry. This may take twenty-four hours or longer.

## Knife-Edge Pillow

A knife-edge pillow with no welting is the most simple of all pillows to finish. You will need fabric for backing the pillow, a sewing machine, scissors, straight pins, needle and thread, stuffing for the pillow, and an uncut ball of yarn or pearl cotton for a twisted cord (the last is optional; see step 5).

STEP 1: After you have blocked the needlepoint piece, set the sewing machine for a fine zigzag stitch and sew around the needlepoint, catching the final row of stitching to the canvas just outside the work. Sew around the needlepoint two or three times. Trim the canvas, leaving approximately ⅝ inch of canvas outside the machine stitching.

STEP 2: Cut the fabric backing to match the size of the needlepoint stitching plus a ⅝-inch seam. Pin the right side of the fabric to the right side of the needlepoint piece.

STEP 3: With the wrong side of the needlepoint facing up, sew the needlepoint to the fabric backing. Sew into 1 row of the needlepoint stitching, just inside the zigzag stitching. Do not sew all four sides closed; leave an opening at the bottom of the pillow just large enough to turn the pillow. Clip the fabric at each corner on a diagonal to reduce the amount of fabric slightly.

STEP 4: Turn the pillow so that the right sides of the needlepoint and fabric are facing out. Fill the pillow firmly with stuffing. Turn under the open seams at the bottom of the pillow and hand-sew the flap closed. If you want to add a twisted cord (step 5) to the pillow, do not sew the flap entirely closed. Leave an opening of approximately ½ inch into which you will tuck the ends of the cord.

STEP 5: (*Optional*) If you want to add a twisted cord to the pillow, cut 4 strands of yarn measuring twice the distance around the pillow plus 6 inches. Make the cord according to the directions under Twisted Cords. Note that one end of the cord has a finished round end while the other has a group of raw strand ends. Begin with the round end. Leaving a tail approximately 1 inch long, attach the cord to the pillow at point A on Figure 75. Following the direction of the arrows indicated, sew the cord to the pillow, ending at point B. The cord will be slightly too long. Cut, rewrap, and retie the cord with thread, leaving a tail approximately 1 inch. Tuck the two tails into the small opening at the bottom of the pillow and sew the opening closed.

## Glasses Case

To make a glasses case, you will need the following supplies: fabric for lining, scissors, straight pins, needle and thread, 3 strands of yarn or pearl cotton twice the measurement following the pattern of Figure 77 plus 6 inches, 1 skein of yarn or pearl cotton for a small tassel.

STEP 1: After you have blocked both needlepoint pieces, cut two pieces of lining the same size as the needlepoint plus ⅝ inch. You will work on one needlepoint piece and one lining piece; put the second needlepoint piece and lining piece aside. With the wrong sides of the needlepoint and lining pinned together, turn under the seams of each and hand-sew the lining to the needlepoint.

Now repeat this, sewing the second piece of lining to the second piece of needlepoint. This time leave a small opening approximately ½ inch at the base of the top left diagonal into which you will later tuck the end of the cording.

STEP 2: Put together the two sides of the glasses case so that the right sides of the needlepoint face outward. Sew the sides together, catching first a needlepoint stitch on one side and then a needlepoint stitch on the other side. Beginning at point A on Figure 76, sew around three sides of the glasses case, ending at point B. This leaves the top diagonals and the top edge open.

STEP 3: Make a twisted cord following the directions under Twisted Cords. Notice that one end of the cord has a finished round end while the other has a group of raw strand ends. Begin with the round end. Holding the glasses case so that the second piece of needlepoint with the small opening at the base of the diagonal is behind the first piece of needlepoint, sew the round end of the cord to the glasses case at point A on Figure 77. Following the direction of the arrows indicated on Figure 77, sew the cord to the glasses case, ending at point B. The cord will be slightly too long. Cut, rewrap, and retie

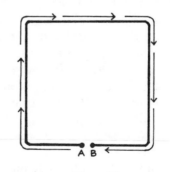

*Figure 75*

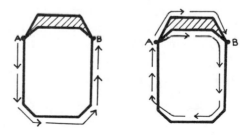

*Figure 76*          *Figure 77*

199

the cord with thread, leaving a tail approximately ½ inch. Tuck the tail into the small opening and sew the opening closed.

STEP 4:   Attach a small tassel with a wrapped or webbed head to the bottom of the glasses case. See the instructions under Basic Tassels, Wrapped Tassel Heads, and Webbed Tassel Heads.

## Bell Pull

To finish a bell pull you will need the following supplies: fabric for backing the needlepoint, a sewing machine, scissors, straight pins, needle and thread, bell pull hardware or a brass bar slightly wider than the bell pull, several skeins of pearl cotton for trimming the top, and a tassel for the bottom.

STEP 1:   After you have blocked the needlepoint piece, set the sewing machine for a fine zigzag stitch and sew around the needlepoint, catching the final row of stitching to the canvas just outside the work. Sew around the needlepoint two or three times. Trim the canvas, leaving approximately ⅝ inch of canvas outside the machine stitching.

STEP 2:   Cut the fabric backing to match the size of the needlepoint stitching plus a ⅝-inch seam. Pin the right side of the fabric to the right side of the needlepoint piece.

STEP 3:   With the wrong side of the needlepoint facing up, sew the needlepoint to the fabric backing. Sew into 1 row of the needlepoint stitching just inside the zigzag stitching. Do not sew all four sides closed. Leave an opening at the bottom of the bell pull just large enough to turn the bell pull. Clip the fabric at each corner on a diagonal to reduce slightly the amount of fabric.

STEP 4:   Turn the bell pull inside out so that the right sides of the needlepoint and fabric are facing out. Turn under the open seams at the bottom of the bell pull and hand-sew the flap closed.

STEP 5:   Attach traditional bell pull hardware or trim the bell pull using the following directions.

## Bell Pull Top Trim (1)

(For the Chinese Garden bell pull) Divide the top of the bell pull into equidistant points as in Figure 78. Starting at point B on Figure 78, make a 1½-inch loop with a single strand of pearl cotton threaded on a needle. Leave a long tail before you begin. Continue sewing through the bell pull until the loop is 4 threads, then remove the needle from the pearl cotton end. You now have two long tails of pearl cotton. See Figure 79.

Beginning at the base of the loop, make macramé half-knot twists around the loop threads, allowing the knots to twist as you work. When you have worked half-knot twists all around the loop, thread each tail on a needle and run the tail through the center of the knots about 1 inch to conceal it. Bring out the end and cut it close to the knots. Repeat this, making loops at points C through F. When you have finished, you will have five loops. See Figure 80.

Thread 3 strands of pearl cotton, each approximately 30 inches long, through the bell pull at point A. Doubled over, the 3 strands become 6 strands, each approximately 15 inches long. See Figure 81. Using 2 strands, make a series of macramé knots around 4 strands until you have a rope approximately 7½ inches long. Tie an overhead knot, and leaving a 4-inch tail of thread ends, clip the strands. Repeat this, making a 7½-inch rope at point G. You now have five loops and two ropes along the top of the bell pull. See Figure 82.

Using Method 2 as described under Basic Tassels, add a tassel to each rope tail. Make a wrapped tassel head for each tassel following the instructions under Wrapped Tassel Heads.

Finally, slip the brass bar through the loops. Wrap the end ropes around the bar, allowing the tassels to hang along each side of the bell pull. See Figure 83. When you have completed the top trimming of the bell pull, make a large tassel according to the instructions under Tassel with Needleweaving and attach the tassel to the bottom of the bell pull.

## Bell Pull Top Trim (2)

(For the Chinese Butterflies bell pull) Starting at point A on Figure 84, make a 1½-inch loop with a single strand of pearl cotton threaded on a needle. Leave a long tail before you begin. Continue sewing through the bell pull until the loop is 4 threads, then remove the needle from the pearl cotton end. You now have two long tails of pearl cotton. See Figure 79.

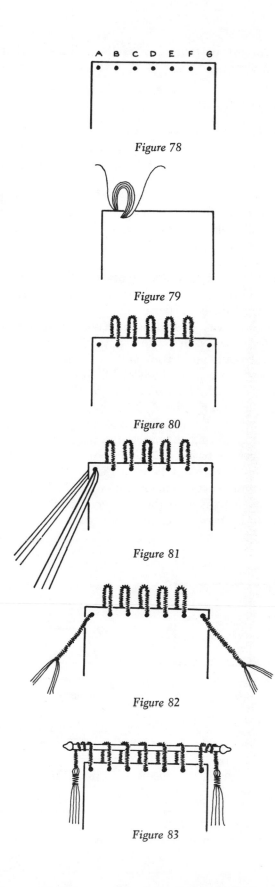

Figure 78

Figure 79

Figure 80

Figure 81

Figure 82

Figure 83

Beginning at the base of the loop, make macrame square knots around the loop threads. When you have worked square knots all around the loop, thread each tail on a needle and run the tail through the center of the knots about 1 inch to conceal the end. Bring out the end and cut it close to the knots.

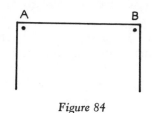

Figure 84

Repeat this, making a second loop at point B on Figure 84. You will now have two loops. Slip a brass bar through the two loops. When you have completed the top trimming for the bell pull, add a fringe to the bottom. See the following instructions.

## Bell Pull Fringe

To make a fringe for a bell pull, you will need approximately two to three balls of pearl cotton, scissors, and a tapestry needle with an eye sufficiently large to hold the pearl cotton.

STEP 1: Cut an odd number of pearl cotton strands, each approximately 40 inches long. Thread each strand through the bottom edge of the bell pull from right to left and double it. Space the strands approximately ⅛ to ¼ inch apart.

Cut another strand approximately 100 inches long and thread it through the bottom left point on the bell pull edge so that one part of the strand equals in length the other strands and the second part of the strand is approximately four times the length of the other strands. See Figure 85.

STEP 2: Using the long strand as the carrying thread, place it from left to right across the other strands. Knot each strand around the carrying thread using a double half-hitch knot. Work from left to right. When you have knotted a whole row, place the carrying thread from right to left across the other strands and make a series of double half-hitch knots from right to left. You now have two rows of double half-hitch knots.

STEP 3: Working from the left, pick up 4

strands and make two square knots. Drop these 4 strands, pick up 4 more strands, and make two more square knots. Repeat this, working across the fringe until you have a series of two square knots.

Returning to the left side, leave the first 2 strands in place. Pick up the next 4 strands and make two square knots. Drop these strands, pick up the next 4 strands, and make two more square knots. Continue across the fringe.

Returning to the left side, pick up the first 4 strands and make two square knots. Drop these strands, pick up 4 more strands, and make two more square knots. Continue across the fringe. When you finish, you will have three rows of alternating square knots.

STEP 4: Return to the left and pick up the long carrying thread. Place it from left to right across the fringe and knot a row of double half hitches as in step 2.

Place the carrying thread from right to left across the fringe and knot a second row of double half hitches as in step 2.

STEP 5: Divide the fringe into groups of 12 strands. If the fringe does not divide exactly evenly, recalculate and distribute the remaining strands 1 to each group. Pick up the first group of strands. Using 4 strands on the left and 4 on the right, make three square knots around the 4 center strands. Tie an overhand knot of all strands and let the ends hang loosely. Repeat this, making three square knots and an overhand knot for each group of strands.

Then cut the bottom edges of the strands so that they are even.

## Purse with Needlepoint Top

(Mongol and Chinese purses) When you have completed stitching the purse design, you will have four pieces of needlepoint: two for the purse top and two for the purse body. Block all four pieces.

To make the purse, you will need the following supplies: fabric for lining the purse, scissors, straight pins, needle and thread, a sewing machine, and approximately three skeins of pearl cotton for making two twisted cords.

STEP 1: After you have blocked all four purse pieces, trim the excess canvas, leaving a ⅝-inch seam. Cut lining for each purse piece the size of the needlepoint plus a ⅝-inch seam. You will work first with one needlepoint purse top and its lining and one needlepoint purse body and its lining. Set aside the other purse top and body and their linings.

STEP 2: With the wrong side of the purse top facing the wrong side of its lining, pin the two pieces together. Turn under the seams along the left and right edges and hand-sew the needlepoint and lining together from point A to point B and then from point C to point D as in Figure 86. The top and bottom edges remain unfinished. Fold the purse top in half, with the needlepoint facing outward, and baste together the raw edges as in Figure 87.

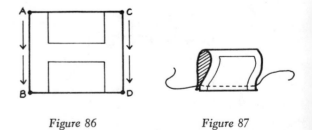

Figure 86          Figure 87

STEP 3: Baste around the purse body 2 rows into the stitching as in Figure 88. This will serve as a guide for seams.

STEP 4: Place the needlepoint purse body right side up in front of you. Place the purse top upside down on the purse body so that the stitching along the raw edges of the purse top matches the stitching along the top edge of the purse body. Center the

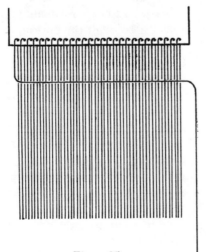

Figure 85

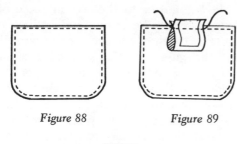

Figure 88          Figure 89

Figure 90

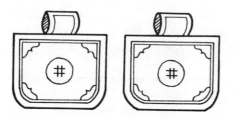

Figure 91

Figure 92

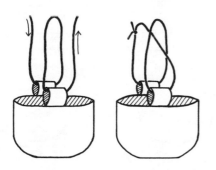

Figure 93          Figure 94

purse top, pin and baste it in place. See Figure 89.

STEP 5: Pin the right sides of the purse body and lining together. With the wrong side of the needlepoint facing up, machine-sew across the top edge of the purse body. Sew along the basting line. You have now attached the needlepoint and lining across the top edge of the purse, catching the purse top in place between the two. Reinforce the edge by machine-sewing across the top twice more.

STEP 6: Turn the needlepoint and lining so that the wrong sides face each other and the top pops up. Pin the lining to the needlepoint. Turn under the seams and hand-sew the lining to the needlepoint. Leave a small opening approximately ½ inch at point A on Figure 90. You will later tuck the end of the twisted cord into this opening.

STEP 7: Using the second purse top and lining and the second purse body and lining, repeat steps 2 through 5. You have now completed two purse halves as in Figure 91.

STEP 8: With the right sides of the needlepoint facing outward, hand-sew the two purse halves together, along three sides from point A to point B as indicated by the arrows in Figure 92. Take care not to sew closed the small openings left for the twisted cord ends.

STEP 9: Cut 4 strands of pearl cotton measuring approximately twice the distance from A to B on Figure 92 plus 6 inches. Make a twisted cord following the directions under Twisted Cords.

Note that there are small openings between the needlepoint and lining at both points A and B. Leaving a tail approximately ½ inch, attach the round finished end of the twisted cord just below the small opening at point A. Sew the cord to the purse edge, following the direction of the arrows on Figure 92 and ending just below the small opening at point B.

The cord will probably be longer than you need. Leave ½ inch of cord plus a small tail, then rewrap, retie, and clip the cord. Tuck each cord end into the small opening near it and sew each opening closed.

STEP 10: Cut 8 strands of pearl cotton each 48 inches long and make a twisted cord following the instructions under Twisted Cords. Slip the cord through the purse tops as illustrated in Figure 93. Knot the two ends of the cord, as in Figure 94, and pull the cord until the knot is concealed in one of the purse tops.

## Purse with Bone Handles

(Tibetan purse) When you have completed stitching the purse design, you will have three pieces of needlepoint: two for the purse body and one for the purse gusset. Block all three pieces. To make the purse you will need the following supplies: one pair of bone purse handles approximately the width of the purse, lining, scissors, straight pins, needle and thread, four ½-inch beads with fairly large holes, approximately four skeins of pearl cotton for twisted cords and tassels, and 2 strands of contrasting pearl cotton for wrapping tassel heads.

STEP 1: After you have blocked all three purse pieces, check the measurement of the gusset against the purse body. The gusset should fit around three sides of the purse body, starting and ending approximately 1 inch below the top edge of the purse. See Figure 24.

Trim the excess canvas from each needlepoint piece, leaving a ⅝-inch seam. Cut lining for each piece to the size of the needlepoint plus a ⅝-inch seam.

STEP 2: You will work first with one piece of the purse body and its lining. Set the other pieces aside. With the wrong side of the needlepoint facing the wrong side of the lining, pin the lining to the purse body. Turn under all seams and hand-sew the needlepoint and the lining together. Leave a small opening approximately ½ inch at both points A and B as in Figure 95. You will later tuck the ends of the twisted cord into these small openings.

Repeat this step, using the second purse body and lining, again leaving ½-inch openings at points A and B as in Figure 95.

With the wrong sides of the gusset and lining together, fold under all seams and hand-sew the lining to the gusset. Now all three needlepoint pieces are attached to lining and all raw edges are turned under.

STEP 3: Taking one piece of the purse body and the gusset, pin the gusset along three sides of the purse body, beginning and ending approximately 1 inch below the top edge of the purse. See Figure 24. Hand-sew the gusset to the purse body, catching first a needlepoint stitch on one side and then a needlepoint stitch on the other side.

Now pin the gusset to the second piece of the purse body, carefully beginning and ending at the same places as on the first piece of the purse body. Hand-sew the gusset to the second piece of the purse body, again catching first a needlepoint stitch on one side and then one on the other. All three pieces of the purse are now attached. See Figure 96.

STEP 4: Cut 4 strands of pearl cotton measuring approximately twice the distance from A to B on Figure 96 plus 6 inches. Make a twisted cord following the directions under Twisted Cords.

Leaving a tail approximately ½ inch, attach the round finished end of the twisted cord just below the small opening at point A. Sew the cord to the purse edge, following the direction of the arrows on Figure 96 and ending just below the small opening at point B.

The cord will probably be longer than you need. Leave ½ inch of cord plus a small tail, and then rewrap, retie, and clip the cord. Tuck each cord end into the small opening near it and sew the opening closed.

Repeat step 4, adding the twisted cord to the second side of the purse body.

STEP 5: Sew the bone handles to the top edges of the purse at intervals dictated by the holes in the handles.

STEP 6: With a needle and a strand of pearl cotton, catch one purse edge at point A on Figure 97 and the second purse edge at point B. Pull the two ends of the strand of pearl cotton tightly, forcing the two edges of the purse together and creating a fold in the gusset. Sew two reinforcing stitches from A to B, pull them tightly, and then tie a square knot with the two ends of the pearl cotton. See Figure 98.

Slip a bead over the two strand ends. Using

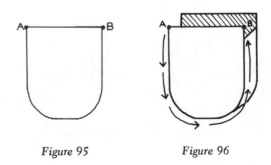

Figure 95          Figure 96

Method 2 under Basic Tassels, attach the tassel to the two strand ends. Then wrap the tassel head following the instructions under Wrapped Tassel Heads.

Repeat step 6 on the opposite side of the purse.

STEP 7: Cut 2 strands of pearl cotton approximately 36 inches each and make a twisted cord according to the instructions under Twisted Cords. Slip the cord through the left holes of both purse handles, dividing the length as follows: the back length of cord should be approximately 22 inches long; the front length should be approximately 14 inches long as in Figure 99.

Measuring 3 inches along the cord from the left holes through which the cord is threaded, tie an overhand knot. Slip two beads over the cord ends and allow them to rest against the knot as in Figure 100.

Slip the long end (21 inches) of the cord through the right holes of the handle from back to front. Carry the long cord up to meet the short cord at a point approximately 3 inches from the right holes of the handles as in Figure 101.

Using both cord ends, tie a knot at this joint. Secure the knot by tugging it until it holds tightly. Clip the ends of the cord very close to the knot. Slip one bead across the top part of the cord chain so that it rests on top of this knot as in Figure 102.

## Finishing Rugs

The primary concern with a rug, unlike most other needlepoint projects except upholstery, is durability. If worked in Tent stitch (another name for Basket-weave or Continental), a rug should withstand years of wear on the floor.

I prefer not to back a rug, but rather to bind the

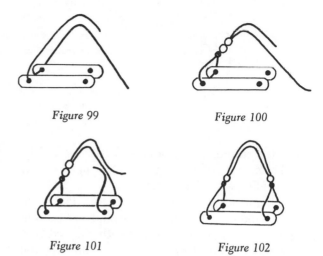

*Figure 99*          *Figure 100*

*Figure 101*          *Figure 102*

edges with rug tape. All fabrics move and adjust in time to atmospheric changes. Two different fabrics bound together will inevitably pull in different directions under stress. Instead of backing the rug, place it on a rug pad. This will give the rug added cushion and yet allow the rug to move freely.

To finish the edges of a rug, you will need a sufficient length of 1-to-1½-inch-wide rug tape to bind all four edges. Buy several additional inches. You may gather up a bit of tape as you sew, and your preliminary measurement may be too short. You will also need scissors, straight pins, and needle and thread.

Block the rug. Clip the excess canvas, leaving a ¾-inch seam. Turn under all seams, also turning under 2 rows of stitching. Pin and baste the seams, mitering each corner. Hand-sew rug tape on top of the seam, catching one edge of the tape to the turned-under rows of stitching and the other edge of the tape to the back of the rug.

## Twisted Cords

To make a twisted cord for a pillow, purse, or glasses case, roll a skein of pearl cotton or yarn into a ball and cut from 2 to 8 strands from the ball, each approximately twice the measurement of the distance around the project plus 6 inches.

Holding one end of the strands, secure the other end to a doorknob. Move away from the doorknob until the strands are stretched fairly taut and begin

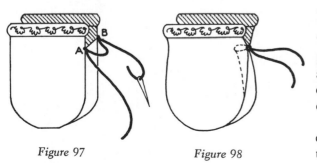

*Figure 97*          *Figure 98*

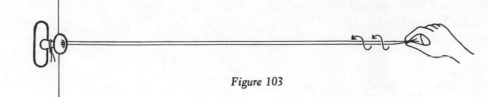

*Figure 103*

to twist the strands in a clockwise pattern. See Figure 103. Continue twisting until the length of the strands is filled with tight twists.

Slacken the length, remove the end attached to the door handle, and double the strands by putting the end you are holding together with the end that was attached to the doorknob. As you do this, the strands will continue to twist. Holding the ends together, smooth the twists so that they fall evenly along the cord.

Note that one end of the cord is a finished, rounded end, while the other is a group of raw strand ends. Wrap and tie thread around the raw strand ends to keep the cord from unraveling.

## Basic Tassels

The procedure for making a tassel depends on how you plan to attach it to a pillow, bell pull, glasses case, and so on. If you wish to make an independent tassel which you will later attach to the corner of a pillow or the end of a glasses case, use Method 1 below.

If you want to add a tassel to the end of an existing tail of yarn or pearl cotton, incorporating these tail strands into the tassel, as with the braid tails on the bell pulls, use Method 2.

METHOD 1:  Cut a square of cardboard slightly larger than the desired length of the tassel. Wrap yarn repeatedly around the cardboard. Slip a separate strand of yarn under the wrapped yarn (see Figure 104) and tie the separate strand tightly around the yarn as in Figure 105. Cut through the strands of yarn at the bottom of the cardboard. You now have strands of yarn hanging from a knotted strand at the top as in Figure 106.

METHOD 2:  Cut a square of cardboard slightly larger than the needed length of the tassel. Wrap yarn repeatedly around the cardboard as illustrated in Figure 107. Cut through the yarn along the bottom edge of the cardboard as in Figure 108 and lift the strands together away from the cardboard. You now have a series of untied strands of yarn as in Figure 109.

Separate the tail strands at the end of a braid as on Bell Pull Top Trim, Figure 82, into two sections. See Figure 110. Fit the tail strands around the tassel strands as in Figure 111 and tie the tail strands tightly below the tassel strands as in Figure 112. You now have strands of tassel yarn and tail yarn mixed together hanging from a braid. Plump the tassel strands around the tail strands to hide the knot as in Figure 113.

## Forming Tassel Heads

The simplest way to form a tassel head is to tie one strand of yarn tightly around the tassel about one third the distance from the top of the tassel. Clip the ends of this strand of yarn so they are the same length as the tassel strands as illustrated in Figure 114.

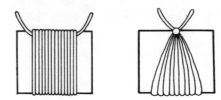

*Figure 104*          *Figure 105*

*Figure 106*

206

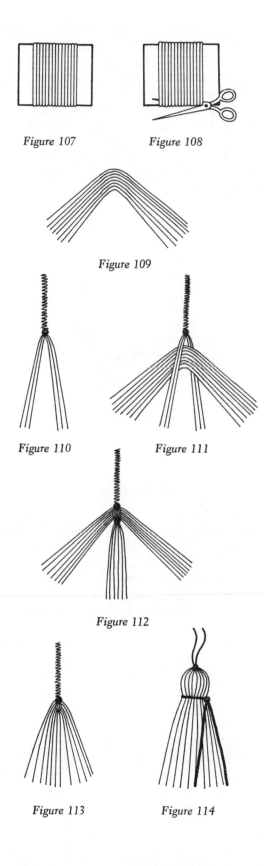

Figure 107

Figure 108

Figure 109

Figure 110

Figure 111

Figure 112

Figure 113

Figure 114

## Wrapped Tassel Heads

For a more decorative tassel head, choose 1 to 3 strands of contrasting yarn and wrap the head of the tassel repeatedly so the wrapping forms a solid block of color. End off one color and add another, or alternate the colors to form a pattern. See the tassels on the bell pulls and glasses cases in Plates 2 and 12.

To wrap a tassel head securely, begin by leaving a long tail and then wrap around this tail as illustrated in Figure 115. To end off one color and begin another, drop the yarn from the first color so that it forms a second tail. Then leave a tail made from the second color yarn and wrap this second color yarn around the tassel strands as well as around the three tails as shown in Figure 116. After a few rows of wrapping, carefully clip the first tail, then the second, and then the third, as in Figure 117.

To end off the wrapping, thread the final tail on a needle. Run the tail through the tassel head to the top and then back down again as in Figure 118. Clip the tail off at the center of the tassel strands.

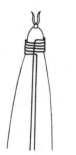

Figure 115

Figure 116

Figure 117

Figure 118

207

## Webbed Tassel Heads

To form a webbed tassel head, tie a strand of contrasting yarn around the tassel about one third of the distance from the top of the tassel, leaving one side of the yarn strand as long as possible. Thread the long side on a needle. (Figure 119.)

With the threaded strand of yarn, make loose loops around the base of the tassel head. (Figure 120.) When you have made loops all the way around the base, begin the second row of webbing by catching the top of the first loop with the needle and making a second loop. (Figure 121.) Continue working around the tassel head, forming new loops until the whole tassel head is covered with webbing. (Figure 122.)

When you reach the top of the tassel, end the yarn by taking 3 little stitches and then pull the needle through the tassel head from top to base. Cut off the yarn at the base of the tassel head and plump the tassel to hide the end.

Return to the base of the tassel head. Thread the short end of the yarn strand tied around the base of the tassel head on a needle and pull the needle through the tassel head to the top and then again to the base. Cut off the yarn and plump the tassel to hide the end.

*Figure 123*

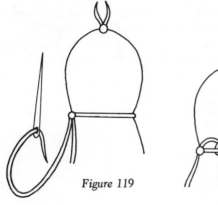

*Figure 119*

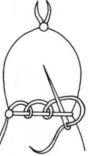

*Figure 120*

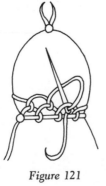

*Figure 121*

*Figure 122*

## Tassel with Needleweaving

(Chinese Garden bell pull) To make a tassel with needleweaving, you will need the following supplies: metal ring 4 inches in diameter, five ½-inch beads with fairly large holes, approximately five to eight balls of pearl cotton, 1 skein of contrasting pearl cotton wound into a ball, several strands of a second contrasting pearl cotton, tapestry needle, and scissors.

STEP 1: Wrap the metal ring with pearl cotton as in Figure 123. When you have wrapped the entire ring, thread the pearl cotton end on a needle and bury the thread end beneath the wrapping about 1 inch. Cut off the remaining end of the strand very close to the wrapping.

STEP 2: Using predominantly horizontal and vertical lines, needleweave with buttonhole stitch the area inside the ring. Add several more lines of needleweaving inside the ring using contrasting pearl cotton. See Figures 124 and 125.

*Figure 124*

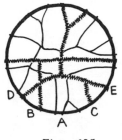

*Figure 125*

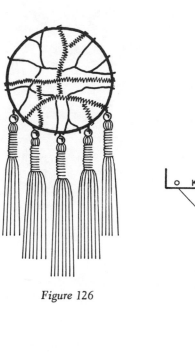

*Figure 126*

*Figure 127*

STEP 3: Double 2 strands of pearl cotton, each 26 inches long, over the ring at point A on Figure 125. When you have doubled the 2 strands, you will have 4 strands. Pull the strands so that the 2 center strands are 12 inches long and the 2 outside strands are 14 inches long. Using the 2 outside strands, tie macrame half-knot twists around the 2 center strands until you have a knotted area approximately ⅜ inch long. Slip one bead over the 4 strands.

Using Method 2 for making a tassel, attach a 10-inch-long tassel below the bead. Wrap the tassel head with the first color of contrasting pearl cotton according to the instructions under Wrapped Tassel Heads. Wrap an area approximately 1 inch long. Using the second color of contrasting pearl cotton, continue wrapping an area approximately another inch long.

Repeat the above at points B and C on Figure 125, making tassels approximately 9 inches long.

Repeat the above at points D and E on Figure 125, making tassels approximately 8 inches long. When you have completed this, you will have five tassels hanging from the wrapped and needlewoven ring. See Figure 126.

STEP 4: To attach the tassel to the bottom of the bell pull, make a 1½-inch loop through the bottom of the bell pull at point A on Figure 127, and around the top of the tassel ring at point B on Figure 127, with a single strand of pearl cotton threaded on a needle. Leave a tail of pearl cotton approximately 11 inches long before you begin. Sew through the bell pull and around the tassel head twice. Remove the needle from the pearl cotton. You now have a 4-strand loop plus two long tails of pearl cotton.

Beginning at the bottom of the bell pull, make macrame half-knot twists around all 4 loop threads to create a single rope. Allow the knots to twist as you work. When you have reached the top of the tassel ring, thread each tail on a needle and run the tail through the center of the knots about 1 inch to bury it. Bring out the end and cut it close to the knot.

Repeat the above, making eight more knotted ropes between points C and D, E and F, G and H, I and J, K and L, M and N, O and P, Q and R in Figure 127. You must increase the length of the loops as you move from the center to the edges.

209

# APPENDIX

*Korean Cranes Pillow*

# STITCH DIAGRAMS

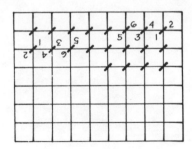

Continental Stitch

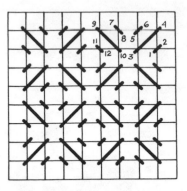

Alternating Mosaic Stitch

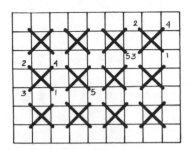

Cross Stitch

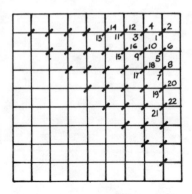

Basketweave Stitch

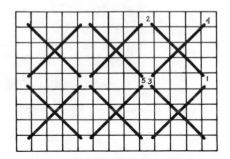

Crossed Corners Stitch—Step 1

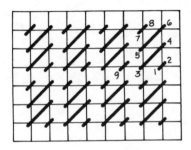

Cashmere Stitch

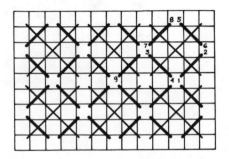

Crossed Corners Stitch—Step 2

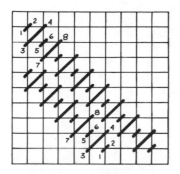

*Diagonal Mosaic Stitch*

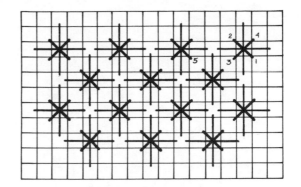

*Double Cross Stitch—Step 2*

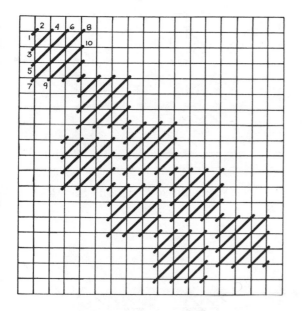

*Diagonal Scotch Stitch*

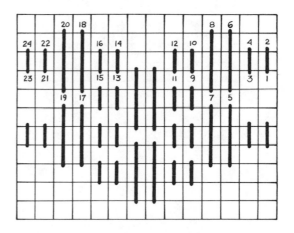

*Double Hungarian Stitch*

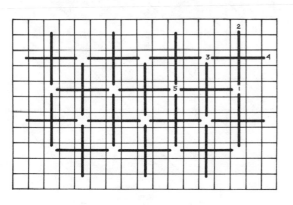

*Double Cross Stitch—Step 1*

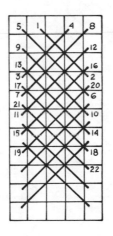

*Fern Stitch*

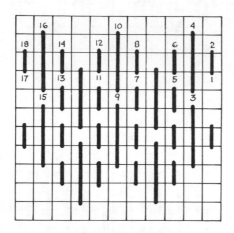

*Hungarian Stitch*

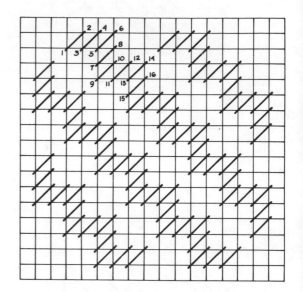

*Jacquard Stitch Variation—Step 1*

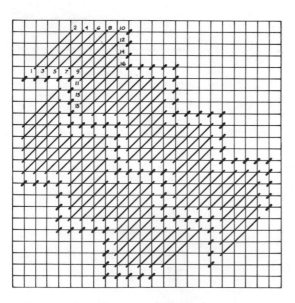

*Jacquard Stitch*

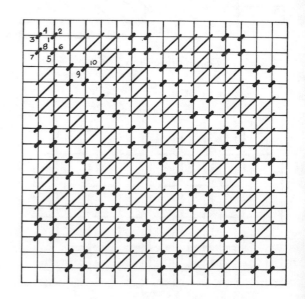

*Jacquard Stitch Variation—Step 2*

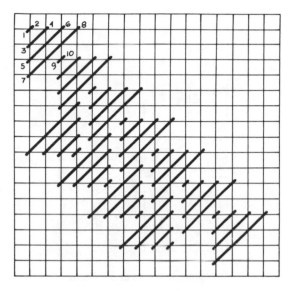

*Milanese Stitch*

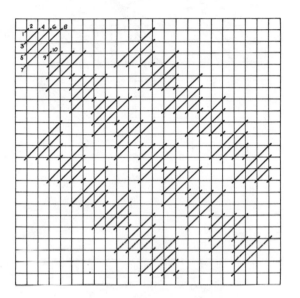

*Oriental Stitch—Step 1*

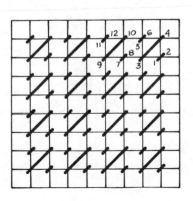

*Mosaic Stitch*

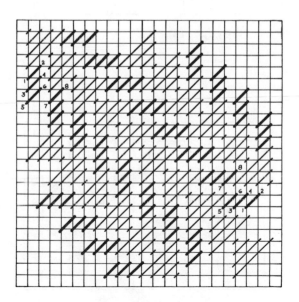

*Oriental Stitch—Step 2*

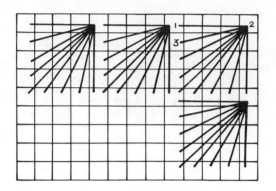

*Ray Stitch*

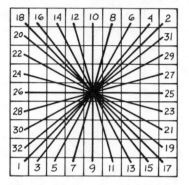

*Rhodes Stitch over 8 Meshes*

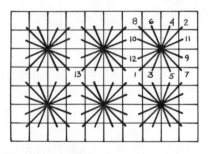

*Rhodes Stitch over 3 Meshes*

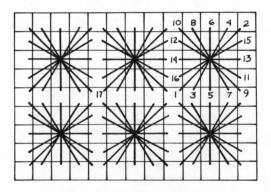

*Rhodes Stitch over 4 Meshes*

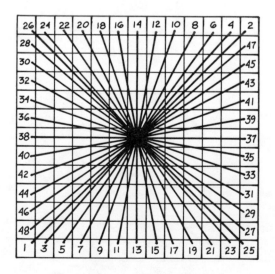

*Rhodes Stitch over 12 Meshes*

216

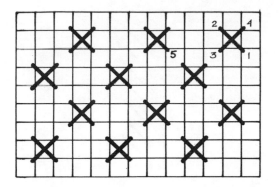

*St. George and St. Andrew Cross Stitch—Step 1*

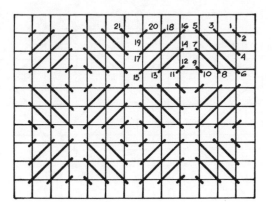

*Scotch Stitch over 3 Meshes*

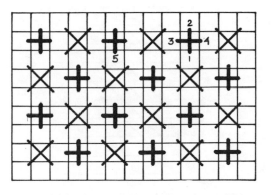

*St. George and St. Andrew Cross Stitch—Step 2*

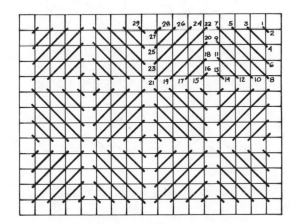

*Scotch Stitch over 4 Meshes*

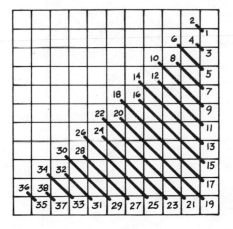

*Satin Stitch*

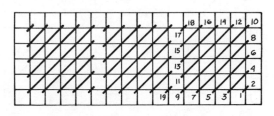

*Scotch Stitch over 5 Meshes*

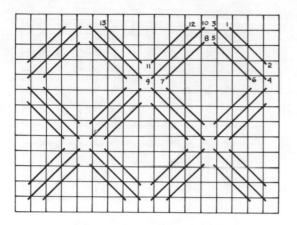

*Scotch Stitch Using Three Colors—Step 1*

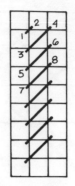

*Slanting Gobelin Stitch over 2 Meshes*

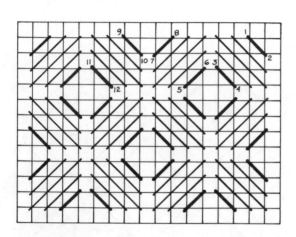

*Scotch Stitch Using Three Colors—Step 2*

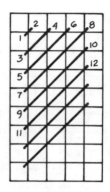

*Slanting Gobelin Stitch over 4 Meshes*

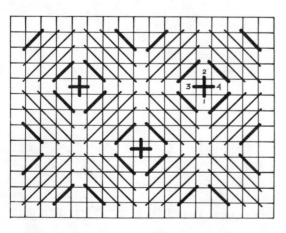

*Scotch Stitch Using Three Colors—Step 3*

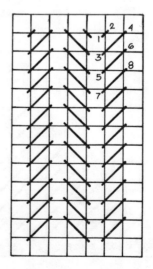

*Slanting Gobelin Stitch Variation*

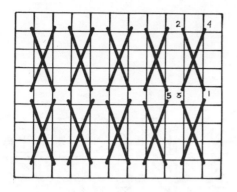

*Tied Cross Stitch—Step 1*

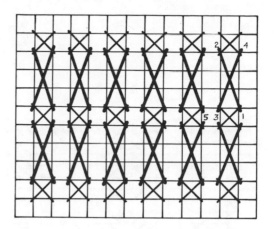

*Tied Cross Stitch Variation—Step 2*

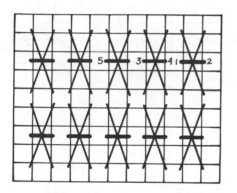

*Tied Cross Stitch—Step 2*

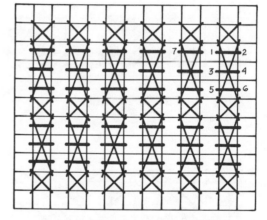

*Tied Cross Stitch Variation—Step 3*

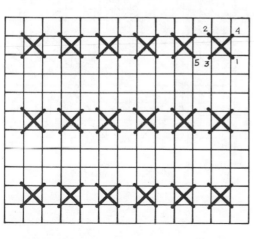

*Tied Cross Stitch Variation—Step 1*

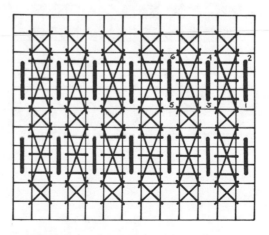

*Tied Cross Stitch Variation—Step 4*

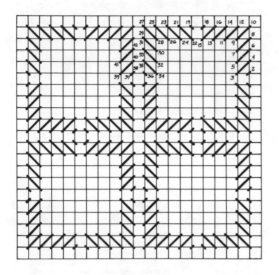

*Tile Stitch—Step 1*

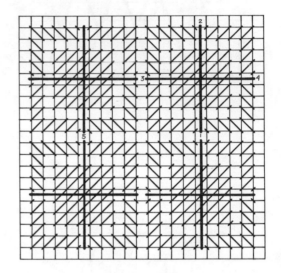

*Tile Stitch—Step 3*

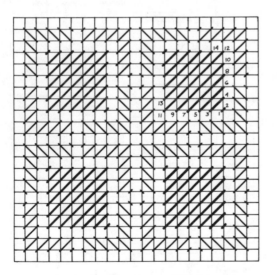

*Tile Stitch—Step 2*

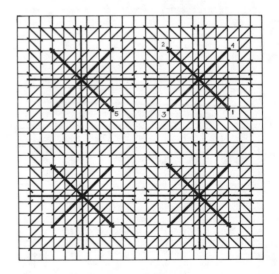

*Tile Stitch—Step 4*

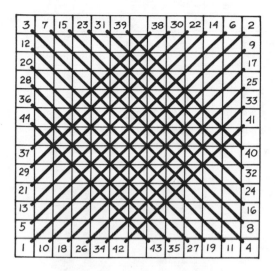

Waffle Stitch over 12 Meshes

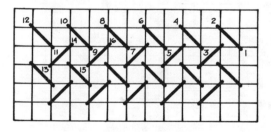

Woven Stitch

Woven Stitch Variation

# ALPHABET

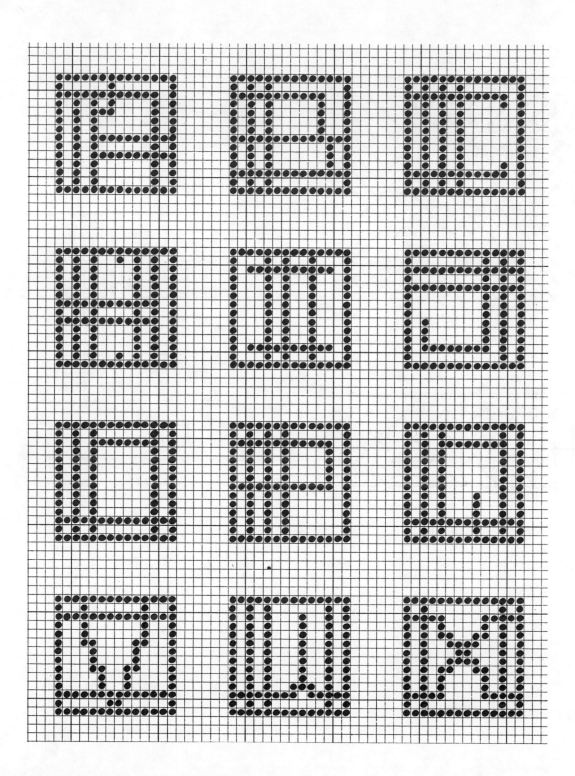

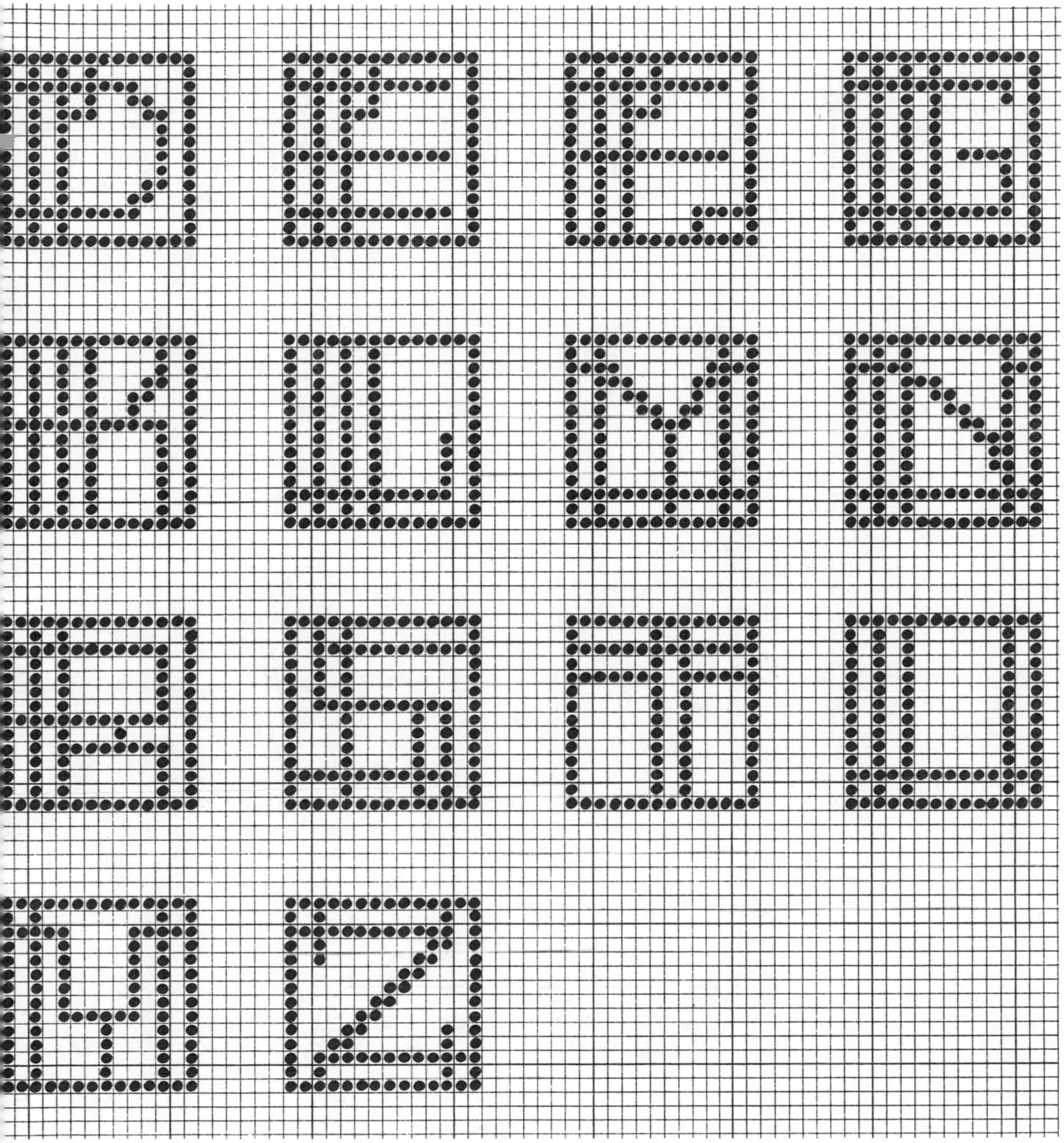

# MACRAME KNOTS

Macrame Square Knot

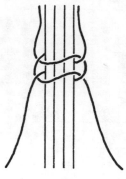

Macrame Half-Knot Twist

Macrame Square Knot Using 12 Strands

Overhand Knot

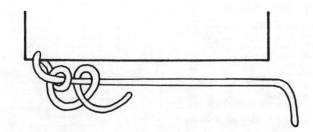

Macrame Double Half-Hitch Knot